Love What Lasts

How to Save Your
Soul from Mediocrity

ALSO BY JOSHUA GIBBS

How to Be Unlucky:
Reflections on the Pursuit of Virtue

Something They Will Not Forget:
A Handbook for Classical Teachers

The 25th:
New and Selected Christmas Essays

Love What Lasts

How to Save Your
Soul from Mediocrity

Joshua Gibbs

CiRCE
CONCORD, NC

Published in the USA
by the CiRCE Institute
© 2023 Joshua Gibbs

ISBN: 979-8-9869172-0-7

For information:
CiRCE Institute
81 McCachern Blvd
Concord, NC 28025
www.circeinstitute.com

Cover design by Graeme Pitman
Layout by David Kern

Printed in the United States of America.

For Paula, whom I swore to love.

Contents

Foreword by Anthony Esolen

Foreword

by Anthony Esolen

In the late summer, on an island in Canada where tourists don't often come, I go to a field I know that is covered with wild blueberries. I will spend several hours each day I visit there, filling a gallon milk pail with the top cut off. I am not there for the experience of it, not if you mean that I have spent a certain amount of time or money in order to procure a thrill. I am there to pick blueberries. Yes, the honk of a heron may come to me from the nearby lagoon, or the flute of a hermit thrush from a thicket of alders, and they are familiar friends. I hear them as you hear the crunch of snow under your boots on a cold and sunny winter day. They are a part of the ordinary music of the world.

I think I am seldom so near to God and my fellow man than when I climb up an escarpment on the other side of the island, probably trespassing on someone's property though no one cares overmuch about it, to gather up what the natives call "foxberries," but the rest of the English world knows as lingonberries, a smaller and more potent form of the cranberry, to be found in fairly dry and exposed places where no trees can grow. It isn't an experience of "Nature," as some commodity, but rather of the quietly ordinary, what Joshua Gibbs in this wise and keen-sighted book calls the "common," as common as a good loaf of bread we can imagine the mother of Jesus baking at the hearth, the bread for the day. So too when Jesus calms our fears about our temporal fortunes, he calls our attention to the "lilies of the field," which in his land might have been like the wild daisies on the dry hilltops of my home in Pennsylvania, or the small wild roses lower down with their sweet and pungent smell, and he said that not even Solomon in all his glory was clothed like one of these. Ordinary, daily; lovely, not garish; common, not "special," as Gibbs defines it, nor "mediocre" either.

Gibbs calls upon us to cast a cold eye on our habits—not our pastimes, such as collecting stamps, or watching birds, but how we consume the time and evacuate it. It will be easy for a Christian to give his conscience a fair grade as he passes the most obvious tests. The Christian may say, "I do not commit adultery," though he probably watches films that eat away at his soul, or he may say, "I do not steal," though he doesn't like to consider too closely how he earns or spends his money. But Gibbs would have us go to our habits in the realm of the good and homely or the grandly beautiful, before we come to good and bad morals, wherein our capacity to fool ourselves seems boundless. What music, reader, have you listened to in the last week? Was any of it what Gibbs calls uncommon, that which has lasted more than a hundred years, and is likely to do so as long as men still have ears to hear? Was any of it what he calls common, that is, the healthy and natural expression of a people's love for harmony and order, embodying ordinary insights about what life really is like? The first may be a Bach oratorio; the second, the Clancy Brothers and Tommy Makem singing the Irish folk song, "Gypsy Rover." Those two, the uncommon and the common, as Gibbs shows, are interinvolved—as we can see from how often the greatest classical composers drink at the common fountain in the village; think of Brahms' Hungarian dances. They are both opposed to the flashy, the mediocre, what is quickly consumed, what cannot last, because it is itself predicated on stinging a subhuman sensorium with ever-fresh and therefore quickly stale excitations. In this sense, pornography, junk food, vegetative scrolling through the internet, and loud thoughtless mantra-ridden from the same brutalist factory down below.

So then, let us be honest with ourselves. I know quite well that my ear, and therefore that part of my soul that should stir in sympathy with great music, has been partly spoiled by bad music, not that I listen to much of the stuff, but that I have not developed the patience to listen to Beethoven. That is a spiritual handicap, a bad limp in the soul, and even though God will not hold me accountable for my failings in this regard, the failing does its harm, and in the general case, it does make us more prone to vice—which is quick and easy—than it builds the muscles for virtue—which is difficult and long in attaining. I read and teach great works of literature, and I have translated some of them into English poetry, but I know also that I must overcome some resistance to read a good book, as I must overcome resistance to spend real time in prayer, rather than giving God the rush. How many good books have you read in the last month? What great books do you have the patience to read?

Have the patience, then, reader, to enter into this book, and to begin to learn why we do not sufficiently Love What Lasts, and not because we are sinners, but because nothing about the world that surrounds us encourages us to do so. Gibbs is correct to note that our problem is not so much the character of the bad movies up with the bad stuff at all, whatever character it may have. Bad "Christian" art bubbles up from the same bad aesthetic swamp as does bad "secular" art. We are, again, not talking about art that fails to attain the heights of a Michelangelo or a Caravaggio. Man cannot live on grandeur alone. He must have the ordinary, too. Every day of the year cannot be Easter, with trumpets blaring. But when the other days are full of the common, the ordinary, the home-made loaf of bread, the wild blueberries, they are as it were suffused with the reflected glory of Easter. The unknown painter who decorated the walls of a medieval church in some Swedish village was not Michelangelo, nor did he pretend to be. But he was good and solid, like bread, the staff of life. We rather feed on the osteoporosis and the dementia of life, what rots the marrow and consumes the brain. You may not be able to imagine yourself reading Paradise Lost. Perhaps not everyone can read that titanic poem. But if you cannot imagine yourself reading Dickens' David Copperfield, or if you have not read such a book in many years, then something is wrong.

The psalmist rejoices when people say to him, "Let us go up to the house of the Lord." God, who is Goodness itself, makes what is good, and all things that come from his hand are beautiful, even when man is slow to recognize it. We are a people peculiarly starved for beauty—for what stirs the soul beyond and beside rational argument. And here, as Gibbs observes, we Christians have failed our young people, as we have put our trust in the "worldview" of Christianity, and thus have failed to treat art as art rather than as ideology; and in this, as he says, there is maybe a nickel's worth of difference between us and ideological secularists and self-styled progressives, a nickel but not a dime. We do not take the imagination seriously, and so we concede that high ground to Satan, who will otherwise have little to do but pick his teeth and watch as the bad art absorbs the young into its ravenous self.

It should not be so. Bad habits may be hard to break. But broken they must be. And what awaits us when, by the grace of God, we have broken them? Good fields of normality, the solid, the daily, the strong; and greatness awaiting nearby, like the mysterious bush that Moses saw, ever flaming and never consumed. Joshua Gibbs shows us some of the ways we may take. Let us not slip the occasion.

Introduction

The modern man is uncomfortably situated between two contradictory beliefs about art. On the one hand, we maintain that taste is profoundly important. On the other hand, we believe that taste is entirely a matter of personal preference, and so judging another man's taste is vulgar and senseless. The second belief is false and the first is true, but we have not grasped *why* artistic taste is so important. In a society that has largely given up on religion, art has taken the place which hymns, the church calendar, the sacraments, and the Word formerly occupied. This claim is true not only for those who have openly quit the faith, but also for those who attend churches wherein the church itself is not presented as an authority and everything it offers is merely a tool which congregants may decide to use on their faith journey—or not.

When I refer to the religious importance which art now holds, I am not only referring to the tens of thousands of people who claimed their religion was "Jedi" on a 2001 census, or to the half million people ordained as "Dudeist priests" who now walk the earth in homage to *The Big Lebowski*. I am also broadly referring to the late emergence of the "fandom," a growing pop culture phenomenon in which communities devoted to TV shows or comic books dogmatically police themselves, enforce numerous orthodoxies, and posit themselves as the antagonists of other online communities. For readers over a certain age, the concept of the "fandom" might seem painfully juvenile and naïve; however, the prolonging of adolescence which Americans have witnessed over the last twenty years means that people in their 30s and 40s now believe that deep loyalty to comic book heroes or cartoon shows is an acceptable framework for life. Setting aside these extremes for a moment, we may observe that even normal people feel they have revealed something quite significant about themselves when they name their favorite film or favorite record. They do not feel the same when they name the church they attend.

When educated Christians hear someone claim that taste is relative—or that anything is relative—they often begin a rebuttal based on the formal rules of logic. Such rebuttals rarely prove persuasive, however, because the belief that taste is relative is not so much a philosophical dogma that has been carefully and precisely sussed out as an honest reflection on the ephemerality of popular culture. We believe taste is relative for two reasons: first, because we believe that whatever is happening now deserves our undivided attention, and second, because whatever is loved and celebrated today will not be around very long. Thus, the modern man is condemned to enjoy whatever art the zeitgeist thrusts in his face. Anyone who believes that what happened long ago is more important (or more interesting) than what is happening now is condemned as a pervert.

It was not always this way, though.

The deification of the present may have begun in the Garden of Eden, when our remote forebears chose immediate pleasure over future glory, but it was the French Revolution which gave a philosophical shape (and theological fervor) to the belief that the past was the enemy of mankind. In the two centuries since the French Revolution, the belief that the past is inherently antagonistic with the present has profoundly damaged nearly every aspect of human life, but especially the realm of art. Before the French Revolution, there was high art and folk art. After the French Revolution, a third kind of art emerged. This third kind of art was not transcendent, for the very concept of transcendence implies that the past has something to offer us—something we desperately need—and that something of the past will definitely last into the future whether we like it or not. The new art was sensual, immensely pleasurable, hilarious, sexy, cool, shocking, and clever. In this book, I refer to the third kind of art as "mediocre."

To a great degree, I grew up on mediocre art: movies that weren't worth watching twice, music that I would be ashamed to listen to ten years later, books that asked nothing of me. I defended mediocre art throughout my 20s on the grounds it was more thoughtful than it appeared and more profitable than inaccessible classics. And then, after having my first child, I suddenly became willing to admit my own bad taste. I spent my 30s reading old books, gazing at old paintings, reviewing the historical events which gave birth to modernity, and questioning everything I believed in my 20s. Thus *Love What Lasts*, written in my early forties, is a synopsis of all the hope and remorse which emerged from reflecting on my youth.

Love What Lasts is a book about the importance of good taste, but it is not written by someone who claims to have succeeded. Rather, it is written by someone who *wants* to have good taste and who recognizes how destructive bad taste can be. While this book is not autobiographical and most of the personal references are contained within the first two chapters, close readers can peer beneath the most biting claims made about popular culture and discern the voice of experience.

I offer this book to anyone who has flipped through a copy of *Paradise Lost* in a bookstore, longingly sighed, "I wish I liked this," and then purchased something more exciting which was published last year. I offer this book to anyone who has tired of knowing that their favorite musicians and authors are utterly opposed to common sense and Christianity. I offer this book to anyone who suffers from the stunted intellect which comes from prolonged exposure to mediocrity, but who wants something better for their own children. Quite possibly, I offer this book to you.

1.
On Film

"Nobody ever went broke underestimating the taste of the American public."
—*attributed to H. L. Mencken*

I intend to write about everything: literature, music, fashion, cuisine, sexuality, the past, the future, ephemerality, ugliness, transcendence, and beauty. I want to describe the omnipresence of mediocrity in American culture and the bizarre course by which Christians have developed both an insatiable hunger for mediocrity and a pathetic theological defense of that hunger. I want to defend common things, average things, normal things, and show how the desire to have a special marriage, special children, and a special church leads to an unstable, unhappy, and meaningless life. And yet, in order to do all this, I must begin with a question that will strike serious readers as quite banal: *Why do Christians love movies so much?*

There is no better place to begin contemplating modern literature, modern music, and the rest of modern culture (taking the word "culture" as broadly as you please) than with a question about movies.

I beg your patience, for if you are anything at all like me, you are a little tired of hearing Christians talk about film, about "gospel themes" hidden in the margins of pornographic television shows, and about Christ figures in comic books. This is not a book about "redeeming culture," however, but about the sort of culture that can redeem us. I do not intend to forge a license for readers to read, watch, and listen to whatever they like under the umbrella of "Christian liberty," but neither will I suggest that clean music and clean films will necessarily do you good. This is a book which teaches a far older, far more demanding standard for determining what is worth our time. This book will ultimately propose a simple standard for evaluating what you watch, what you listen to, even what you wear—a standard that should appeal deeply to Christians while also being rational to anybody who is not offended by common sense. But I have to begin with the question of why Christians love movies so much.

On the one hand, Christians love movies because everyone loves movies, and Christians are not all that different from secularists, agnostics, atheists, or the growing ranks of people who claim to have no religion at all. Christians love movies because movies are entertaining, amusing, alluring, funny, and exciting. Most Americans watch thousands of hours of television and film every year, which means it is easy to talk with friends or strangers about what they have seen lately, whether they liked it, and why. Many people feel they can express their beliefs, priorities, and tastes by talking about what movies and television shows they find good or bad. If a certain person at a party tells you that he attends a Lutheran church, you have not learned much about him. However, if that person says, "I believe *Ordinary People* is the best film ever made," he likely feels he has revealed something terribly significant about himself, and he may even believe his confession entitles him to learn something significant about everyone else.

Cultural Engagement

At the same time that they participate in the general affection for movies, Christians also love movies for reasons that are not shared by secularists, agnostics, atheists, and so forth. Christians think of film as an important part of cultural engagement, which means they not only like to watch movies and talk about them but also to analyze and interpret them deeply, celebrating certain films for having subtly Christian themes while condemning others for having anti-Christian messages. Christians like to have something to say about movies everyone is talking about. Discussing the hidden themes and symbolic meanings in movies makes Christians feel as though they are informed members of society who keep abreast of important things.

Of course, watching movies is an easy and pleasant way of keeping abreast of things. The Christian who wants to keep his finger on the pulse of society is far more likely to do so by seeing the most popular film in the country than by listening to the most popular record or by reading the most popular novel. Watching a popular movie is a bit like watching the news. The news is the news, no matter how sensational, banal, or awful it is, and if the news happens to contain scandalous stories about the sexual foibles of some politician, Christians do not feel guilty or ashamed to follow such stories, for they feel the need to "stay informed." A man has a certain responsibility to watch the news from time to time; in the same way that he ought to know what his children have been up to lately, he ought to know what the president, the Senate, the House of Representatives, powerful corporate executives, and influential celebrities have been up to as well.

Within the last generation, "cultural engagement" has become a popular theological concept that has greatly changed Christian taste in film. The term "cultural engagement" is relatively new, very fashionable, and thus obviously bound for the slag heap of history. In the event that some reader of the distant future has taken up this book, thumbed through the first several pages, and wondered what the expression means, I should say that cultural engagement was a theological trend of the early twenty-first century wherein Christians supposed the real heart of evangelism lay in having both up-to-the-minute knowledge of secular culture and dazzling insights into it. Secular culture was thought to be its own language, and in order to share the gospel, Christians had to speak secular culture fluently. In the same way that residents admire tourists who have learned a little of their native tongue, so, too, unbelievers would be impressed by the humility of Christians who could, say, bring to light the cryptic hunger for God buried in the latest blockbuster. St. Paul said he would "become all things to all men," so in order to reach a generation obsessed with pornographic music and vapid, billion-dollar CGI spectacles, Christian obsessions must follow suit.

Accordingly, many Christians believe that watching a movie is justifiable if they have something interesting to say about it afterwards. The more lurid the movie, the more profound their analysis must be. Thus, a film or television program with grotesque violence and explicit sex must have truly profound gospel themes, although mindless children's shows are vindicated merely because they offer simple moral lessons.

As an alternative, some Christians prefer to reduce a film to its worldview or essential presuppositions. Depending on the plot, the volume of objectionable content, and whether the narrative seems to condemn or condone particular sins, a film might be deemed secularist, nihilist, existentialist, postmodern, pagan, or what have you. Any worldview other than the Christian worldview is judged to be wrong, but provided that the viewer correctly diagnoses the intellectual illness of a film, it poses little problem for the viewer's soul.

While worldview analysts tend to find most films problematic, from time to time a film unwittingly borrows from the Christian worldview and offers something redemptive. If the hero risks his life with his arms outstretched, he can be viewed as a "Christ figure." Or, if a character undergoes a change of heart shortly after getting a barrel of water dumped on his head, the water might be viewed as a kind of baptism and thus the film has "gospel themes."

While some Christians still prefer worldview analysis as a cultural hermeneutic, it has largely been replaced by cultural engagement. With the ascendance of Emergent Christianity in the years following the World Trade Center attacks, worldview analysis fell out of fashion and young Christian essayists and bloggers adopted a softer approach to analyzing secular films. Worldview analysis was more fashionable in the 1990s, but came to be seen as nit-picky, strict, overly intellectual, and overly critical. The worldview analyst wanted to build a hedge of protection around his heart which could keep the world out, but Emergent Christians fancied themselves bridge builders and styled their approach to secular culture as one of deference, sympathy, and respect. Emergent Christians prided themselves on the familiarity and kinship they felt towards the world, even going so far as to claim that the world's complaints against Christianity were an essential aspect of Christianity itself. Whereas the worldview analyst occasionally, begrudgingly admitted Christ figures and gospel themes, sympathetic Christian viewers saw "gospel hunger" everywhere. While worldview analysts were quick to condemn human perversity, the children of worldview analysts saw perverse characters as evidence of "the human need for the gospel." The more perverse, the more clearly our need for the gospel was depicted. Emergent Christians came and went, but their romantic view of "brokenness" remains to this day, and the Emergent definition of cultural engagement became diffuse in American Christianity.

The worldview analyst's tendency to condemn human perversity did not coincide with a reluctance to look at it, however. Worldview analysts were as likely as their Emergent children (I will henceforth call them "sympathists") to watch violent, sexually explicit films, though the former condemned the worldview behind the guts and nipples and the latter exonerated the nipples and guts as a desperate "grasping" for God, as St. Paul put it on Mars Hill.

But the apple does not fall far from the tree. In fact, the worldview analyst and his sympathist son are separated by only a few inches of orchard, for both believe that secular culture warrants a response, and both believe that their own responses to secular culture are an essential part of the so-called Great Commission. The worldview analyst believes his dismantling of secular culture will wow the heathen, and the sympathist believes his friendly, appreciative response to pop music and blockbuster films will prove an educated, diplomatic invitation to secularists. Both think themselves intellectually superior to the films they view, although this prejudice is somewhat justified by the fact that neither viewer has particularly high standards for viewing a film. Both think that there is some intellectual benefit to the viewer in spending time on mediocrity.

The most important thing worldview analysts and sympathists share in common, though, is the absolutely indiscriminate way in which they choose what to watch—and they share this sad trait with nearly all modern men.

Boundless Desire

The way in which modern viewers *choose* what to watch has profoundly changed *what* they watch. Consider the pre-modern world: in ancient Greece, the annual festival of Dionysius provided men with one of few annual opportunities to see a story performed by actors in a theater. In the Middle Ages, the common man lived quite some distance from an operational theater, and was thus never presented with a choice of what to watch. In the early twentieth century, however, moviegoers could enjoy the luxury of choosing between a half dozen motion pictures every weekend. With the popularization of VHS technology in the 1980s, they could choose between hundreds of films at a video store. And with the advent of streaming technology, viewers could choose between tens of thousands of movies, whenever they liked.

While the number of choices increased, movie watching still retained some limitations as long as the choice involved a physical product. As a teenager, I recall indecisively pacing around

the video store for an hour on Friday afternoon, looking for
something which struck me as sufficient entertainment for the
evening; however, once I decided on a particular title, paid for it,
and took it home, I was more or less stuck with it until the following day. When I was a child, it was only with extreme reluctance that my family ever turned off a rented video, and I cannot
recall anyone leaving the house at nine o'clock to get something
else from the video store. Turning off a movie meant that the
evening's entertainment ended early. Thus, renting a video from
a store had a way of securing one's fate for the night: anyone who
rented a video was stuck with it, committed to it, and far more
willing to watch a movie through to the end, simply because
there was no alternative.

By contrast, the era of streaming has created a scenario in
which most viewers have no real commitment to the movies they
begin watching—which is one of many reasons why people have
such a hard time deciding what to watch. Anything we choose
to begin watching can be unchosen five minutes later, at which
point the selection process starts over again. It is hard to choose
when choosing is a meaningless act. It is hard to commit to a film
when the commitment can be easily, painlessly broken.

The act of choosing has also become labyrinthine. In the
1980s, video stores maintained a half dozen sections devoted to
genres like drama and comedy and action, but today's streaming
services are capable of cataloguing films down to very fine nu-
ances of plot. At the time of writing, Netflix had fifteen different
kinds of thrillers, including "steamy thrillers" and "international
thrillers." It also listed more than a dozen different action genres,
two dozen sci-fi genres, and three dozen kinds of comedies. The
proliferation of genres has kept pace with the proliferation of

titles. Just before the demise of video stores, the average Block-buster stocked around seven thousand titles. Today, more than ten times that number are available on Amazon.

As opposed to giving people exactly what they want, the pro-liferation of options has proven disorienting. The average American now spends more than a hundred hours every year browsing Netflix menus.[1] The problem is not just the staggering number of titles to choose from, but also that we have become far harder to please. When my children tell me they are hungry, I tell them they can have an apple. When they tell me they don't want an apple, I say, "Then you're not feeling hungry. You're feeling picky." Given the profound specificity that is now possible in classifying movies, we scroll through endless menus under the delusion that it is possible to find a film which perfectly suits our mood. We do not want to watch something good, but something that flat-ters our feelings and our tastes.

Beginnings

The rather simple thesis of this book came to me several years ago while sitting in a movie theater, waiting for *Jurassic World: Fallen Kingdom* to begin. It was a summer's day. When I bought my ticket, I saw that a film entitled *First Reformed* was playing as well. Several friends had told me that *First Reformed* was a re-markable film, worth seeing, and very moving, but I purchased a ticket for a dinosaur movie instead. As I waited for *Jurassic World* to begin, I tried to imagine how I would explain to a stranger why I had not purchased a ticket for *First Reformed*. I did not expect *Jurassic World* to be any good. I figured that I would walk out of the theater and never give the story a second thought. The film would, I suspected, not offer anything thoughtful or even vaguely philosophical to mull over. I would not need more than thirty seconds to discuss the film with a friend. Rather, I imagined summarizing my feelings about the film as either, "It was better than I thought it would be," or, "It wasn't very good," and then moving on to some more interesting subject. On the other hand, I knew that *First Reformed* would probably be the kind of movie that deserved a second viewing. I knew it was the kind of film I could discuss at length with my friends.

However, the choice wasn't really between *Jurassic World* and *First Reformed*. The choice was between *Jurassic World* and every classic film I haven't seen. A ticket to *Jurassic World* cost twelve dollars, but I might have checked *Cinema Paradiso* out from the library for free. I have never seen *Cinema Paradiso*, but I've heard it is quite good.

I've never seen *The Searchers*, either, or *The Passion of Joan of Arc*, *Battleship Potemkin*, *Late Spring*, *Seven Samurai*, *Persona*, or *Bicycle Thieves*. Some people do not respect film as an art form, but I do, and I believe that watching a good film can help a man's soul move nearer to God. My sanity has been restored many times by great films. Nonetheless, I purchased a ticket for *Jurassic World*. Having considered the possibility of watching *Late Spring* or *Bicycle Thieves* or *First Reformed*, which could have brought me nearer to God, I decided to do what was easier. I chose a blockbuster film that would overwhelm my senses and starve my intellect. It is a choice I have made many, many times.

As a high school teacher, I have heard both teenagers and adults make the case for blockbuster films. The case that the adult makes is nearly indistinguishable from that of the high school student, a fact that ought to make the teenager suspicious and the adult blush. The case for blockbusters largely consists of two entirely incompatible theses. The first thesis is that block-buster films are not nourishing, but neither is candy, and while no one can live on candy, no sane person would try. The second thesis is that blockbuster films are actually far more sophisticated than they appear on the surface.

If blockbusters are actually like candy—nothing more than a diversion, a lark, a trifle—then only a crank would complain about them. However, our society does not treat blockbusters as mere diversions. A kid at a pizza parlor waiting for a takeout order might pass the time by putting a few quarters in a Pac-man arcade game. This is a diversion. If a man watches twenty minutes of *Die Hard* on a hotel television while his wife gets dressed for the evening, this is a diversion. And yet, the release of a blockbuster film is a global event, like a visit from the pope or the assassination of a European archduke. While no blockbuster film actually lingers very long in the American imagination, the adoration of blockbuster films has become one of the chief cultural heirlooms that this generation is passing on to the next.

It was not always this way, though.

A Little Perspective

In 1979, the film *Kramer vs. Kramer* was made for $8 million dollars, grossed $106 million dollars (the highest-grossing film released that year), and won five Academy Awards, including Best Picture and Best Director.[2] The film, which was one of the top-grossing movies of the year, is a PG-rated drama about the ways in which a couple's divorce changes them and harms their young son. By contrast, the 2018 Best Picture winner was *Green*

Book, which was only the thirty-sixth highest-grossing film of the year.[3] In 2017, *The Shape of Water* won Best Picture and was the forty-sixth highest-grossing film of the year.[4] In 2016, *Moonlight* won Best Picture and was the ninety-second highest-grossing film of the year.[5] Simply put, Americans are no longer very interested in films that have been declared to be "the best." Spectacles have come to dominate our taste.

At the same time, the highest-grossing film of the year tends to have a very short life. Take a look at a recent compilation of the twenty-five highest grossing films of all time and you'll find that most were released fairly recently. Obtaining a spot near the top is now relatively easy. Maintaining a spot on the list is difficult. A culture which is based on pure appetite will create an endless supply of products that are staggeringly and profoundly popular, but only for a little while. Like the sugar rush that comes from candy, the pleasure of the film fades quickly but leaves a taste for something equally sweet.

The second thesis that is often used to defend blockbusters is that they are actually more sophisticated than they appear. While this thesis is at odds with the first, it is the more common of the two and the more widely accepted. Comic book films now receive scholarly attention, long and nuanced reviews, and the same degree of critical scrutiny formerly reserved for films marketed to honest-to-God adults. It is not uncommon (or considered strange) for a review of *Deadpool* or *Batman* to discuss what the film has to say about America's international policy, universal health care, capitalism, climate change, race, gender, or a dozen other issues about which the director has no competence to speak.

At the same time, it is perfectly understandable that the filmmakers would feel compelled to say something about important matters—after all, many blockbusters now cost hundreds of millions of dollars to make, rake in over a billion dollars, and bring more people to theaters in a month than will go to church during that time. Little nods to "significant issues" add the illusion of profundity and make moviegoers feel as though they are not wasting their time. What is more, reviews of comic book films often invoke fashionable, unreadable modern philosophers like Derrida, Hegel, and Foucault, which flatters viewers into thinking that a refined intellect is necessary in order to truly understand what is nothing more than a gazillion-dollar special effects bonanza. The average *Avengers* viewer has never read Foucault, though, which means that a blockbuster also needs a few easy themes and archetypes, and so the final act of a blockbuster usually centers on sacrifice or teamwork—teamwork if it is an ensemble piece, sacrifice if it is a one-man show.

Granted, many of the critics who treat blockbuster films as compelling, rewarding works of art are well-read, thoughtful individuals, and dismissing all these critics, all their reviews, and every blockbuster film ever made would be immodest and irresponsible. Nonetheless, I will point out that blockbuster films are now quite common (as are glowing reviews) and if half these films are as good as anyone claims, we could expect them to linger in the cultural imagination for some time—but they don't. Our interest in blockbusters swells suddenly, then dies down as suddenly as it came. *It's a Wonderful Life* barely broke even at the box office, but because the film is so good, it still plays in theaters all over the world every December, seventy-five years later. Blockbuster films, on the other hand, enjoy a three-month theatrical run and are wildly popular for several weeks after they become available for home viewing but more or less disappear by the end of the following year. For the moment, my contention is a rather simple one: if these films were good, they would last a good bit longer.

The fact that lately-released films pass through our cultural digestive system so quickly also means that no one who writes about them has had much time to think about them. While the critic who references Foucault in his review of the latest Marvel film sounds quite impressive, his opinions of his subject have nevertheless been formulated quickly. Social media incentivizes hasty reactions over opinions which are the result of multiple viewings, numerous conversations with friends, and slow ruminations.

Because Christian worldview analysts and sympathists alike see film as an opportunity for cultural engagement, the rapidity with which entertainment is devoured is not thought to be problematic. The worldview analyst can quickly dismantle a film by revealing the philosophical incoherence of the plot and themes, then demonstrate all the ways in which a biblical worldview offers unshakable answers to questions which secular filmmakers can only guess at. Meanwhile, the sympathist can also swiftly reduce a film to a series of unwitting references to the gospel and unfulfilled longings which only Christ can satisfy. Both believe that a film viewing should be followed by recognition of all the philosophical faults and theological inconsistencies, and both regard movies as invitations to talk.

I am being critical, but despite the derogatory way in which I have characterized both kinds of viewers, I believe that the worldview analyst and the sympathist separately understand something vital about the role of the viewer will also failing to get to the heart of the matter. The worldview analyst's blithe condemnation of movies is often justified, but most movies are not worth watching in the first place and watching films which one suspects are unworthy is foolish, pretentious, and slothful. The sympathist rightly understands that some films deserve the benefit of the doubt, but he gives this benefit in a recklessly profligate manner. Both lack a sound rationale for choosing what to watch.

I write this as someone who thought himself a competent worldview analyst for many years, then thought himself a daring sympathist for many years, and then slowly discovered by teaching classic literature that neither position held much water. Having grown up in a Reformed community during the 1990s, I was fully trained in the art of worldview analysis by the time I began college. During college, like most young Christians, I turned against many of the precepts upon which I had been raised and fell in with the fashionable philosophies of the day. I was entranced by the Emergent church and made several pilgrimages to Seattle where I attended Mars Hill services. As I listened with rapture to sermons wherein biblical principles were illustrated with ideas borrowed from secular music and films and observed the fashionable band posters which inexplicably hung in the narthex of the church building, I suddenly felt that my years of devotion to popular culture had not been wasted. I started a blog and spent my early twenties arguing that violent movies and rock music could be spiritually illuminating if only one had the eyes to see it.

At the time when I began arguing that violent movies and rock music were actually profound, I am not sure I had read any old books from front to back. I had attended a classical high school where I prided myself on my ability to write convincing essays on books I had skimmed. In my defense—and it is not much of a defense, I will admit—worldview analysis does not really reward the time and work it takes to do a close read, so I never felt all that guilty for blowing through a thousand lines of Homer in ten minutes. I was able to draw the proper conclusions, and within a community which thought that worldview analysis is a strong hermeneutical strategy, the proper conclusions were usually good enough for a passing grade. When I played the part of the sympathist and wrote impassioned essays advocating for violent films and rock music, I found that the same specious lines of reasoning with which I had learned to condemn a film's worldview could just as easily be used to exonerate it.

It was not until I began my career as a classical literature teacher that I understood the place of the audience and that great works of art invite us to listen, not to talk. At the beginning of my career, my objection to worldview analysis was that it put the audience in an adversarial relationship with the artifact being analyzed. It often seemed that the worldview analyst would do just as well to spend five minutes reading a synopsis of a film as to spend two hours watching it, given the narrow range of qualities and plot points that he found relevant. Were adulterers punished in the end? Were theft and murder condemned? Were sinners unhappy? Did the righteous receive justice? Most of the worldview analyst's task rests on getting simple, objective answers to questions like these, all of which can be found with a quick Google search.

As my career as a teacher of classical literature was beginning, I became the editor of a film review website called FilmFisher. During the first three years that FilmFisher was up and running,

I wrote nearly one hundred film reviews. Very quickly, I discovered that reviews of new films needed to be published within several days of their release. New films that were not reviewed until two or three weeks after their release date would attract little or no readership. Consequently, I would often attend a film on opening night, begin writing the review directly afterward, finish the review on Saturday afternoon, and publish it Saturday evening or Sunday morning. Many of these reviews were little more than exercises in style. As opposed to deciding *how* to say what I believed to be true of a film, I often wrote reviews while still deciding what the truth was. Eventually, the turnaround time between viewing a movie and writing the review seemed so brief that I often began composing a review in my head before the film was over, which turned moviegoing into a chore.

During the first few years in which I wrote for FilmFisher, I believed that a position of lenience and generosity toward a work of art was necessary to truly understand it. However, at the same time that I was writing generous film reviews, I was also teaching Dante and Jane Austen, and eventually I came to the rather obvious conclusion that it was unreasonable to grant the same hearing to *Transformers 3* that I offered to *The Divine Comedy*. Some art warrants a generous audience and some art does not. A book which has survived a seven-century-long vetting process and boasts universal acclaim cannot be evaluated on the same terms as a blockbuster film wherein a lingerie model doubles as an actress and alien robots destroy a major U.S. city. It is foolish to interpret ephemeral and sensual amusements in the same teachable, receptive frame of mind that is deserved by deathless works of art.

It was also problematic to carry the perspective of the moviegoer into the reading of great books. The worldview analyst usually regards himself as the one who must be pleased, but it is arrogant to uncritically dismiss the countless and varied audiences who have claimed for hundreds of year that a certain work is beautiful, true, and humane—and to instead demand that a sacrosanct epic poem prove itself anew.

In the last year, I have delivered a lecture titled "How to Watch a Movie" on two separate occasions, and I opened both lectures by saying, "I would like to teach you how to watch a movie. The first point I would like to make is the most important one, really, and it is this: Don't watch a movie. You watch too many movies."

This point is not entirely in jest. The reason why the average American spends a hundred hours every year scrolling through menus on Netflix (to say nothing of Amazon Prime, Hulu, or Disney+) is that an evening spent in front of the television is often predicated on the claim, "I am in the mood to watch something." When a man begins scrolling through Netflix screens looking for "something," he quickly realizes that he is not *actually* in the mood to watch "something" because every screen he passes over contains half a dozen somethings which he could watch. Neither is the man looking for "something good" to watch, because he knows the titles of fifty classic films he has never seen and is not tempted by any of them. There is a zero percent chance that someone who begins searching for "something to watch" will end up sitting through all of Ingmar Bergman's *Wild Strawberries*.

Rather, the man "in the mood for something" will look for a film which is exciting, sexy, or funny, not something contemplative. He takes up the task of choosing a film with no forethought, no plan, and thus no sense of duty or obligation. By the same token, the man who goes to the cupboard because he wants "something" to eat will usually end up eating chips. When we think of what we *ought* to eat, we think of fruits and vegetables, and the man who enters the kitchen having decided in advance what he will eat is probably going to have an apple. No one thinks they ought to eat chips when they are hungry. When a man buys chips at the store, he tells himself, "I'll have a few of these with a sandwich or a bowl of soup." He does not plan to eat the entire bag in a single sitting, but he could very easily find himself doing this very thing after walking into the kitchen with no plan, no "should," no purpose. Similarly, the man who begins searching for "something"—be it a film, a snack, or a sexual partner—without first clearly defining what standards will guide his search usually ends up deciding with his stomach, not his mind or heart. I will return to this point at the close of this book, but for now I will admit that over the last year, I have watched servile trash like *Armageddon*, *Zoolander*, and *The Hangover*, but only after scrolling aimlessly through a thousand other options. These are not films which any dignified adult would make plans to watch many hours in advance, but rather concessions reluctantly made to an evening which is rapidly disappearing in the mire of indecision.

I should further clarify I have *begun* watching *Armageddon*, *Zoolander*, *The Hangover*, and other such films. I rarely finish them. Rather, I watch one of these films for about an hour, then quit because it is late—and it is late because I have already spent half an hour trying to decide what to watch.

Having spent the last fifteen years teaching at Christian high schools, testimonial evidence suggests that Christians are no better than secularists at choosing what to watch and that regardless of the high-minded reasons they give for watching movies, at the end of the day, what most Christians want is something pleasurable that flatters the senses. Given the extraordinary amount of time that Christians spend watching movies and television, to approach movies and television in an arbitrary fashion—without a plan, without a coherent philosophy, without an eye toward greater maturity and nobility—is to approach a good deal of life as a whole in an arbitrary fashion.

While books, lectures, and essays about better time management have become fashionable in an age of endless distraction, simply watching fewer banal movies is not a sufficient plan. The man who watches one banal movie has very little reason not to watch another, for he has already proven to himself that his time is worth very little. It is possible for a man to manage his time evenly—not spending too much time on any one thing, but thoughtfully portioning hours for work, reading, eating, films, music, conversations with friends, and time spent with his family—and for his life to be nonetheless frittered away in trivialities, for the world is inundated with trivial books, stupid music, empty conversations, and shallow people. Many time management experts claim their services can help distracted people accomplish all the things they really want to do, and yet, unless people want good things, helping them fulfill their desires will only further their destruction.

Taste

As I stated at the beginning of this chapter, it is not my intention to write a book about movies but about literature, music, fashion, cuisine, sexuality, the past, the future, ephemerality, ugliness, transcendence, and beauty. I want to talk about taste, and my contention is that good things are hard to like and good taste is hard to acquire. I have begun a book about acquiring good taste with a series of observations about movies because Americans spend so much time watching movies and television programs. The specious claims Christians make about why we watch movies and the arbitrary, selfish ways in which we choose what to watch have corrupted our taste, for we have an insatiable appetite for things that we know will not last.

While bad taste in film is hardly the worst of our problems, it is emblematic of our bad taste in theology, philosophy, morals, ethics, literature, fashion, and music. Bad taste is cancerous and is rarely contained in a single organ, and good taste is like yeast, for it also tends to spread. I am not suggesting that anyone should begin rebuilding his tastes—his loves, affinities, and prejudices—around movies, but, rather, that the mainstream of American culture is hell-bent on mediocrity and that unless a man makes a conscious effort to swim against the current, he will unintentionally squander his life. Unexamined tastes are not worth indulging. Unexamined desires are not worth satisfying.

Endnotes

1. Angela Moscaritolo, "Netflix Users Waste Ton of Time Searching for Something to Watch," PC. July 21, 2016, https://www.pcmag.com/news/netflix-users-waste-ton-of-time-searching-for-something-to-watch (accessed June 10, 2020).

2. "Domestic Box Office for 1979," *Box Office Mojo*. https://www.boxofficemojo.com/year/1979/ (accessed January 30, 2023).

3. "Domestic Box Office for 2018," *Box Office Mojo*. https://www.boxofficemojo.com/year/2018/ (accessed January 30, 2023).

4. "Domestic Box Office for 2017," *Box Office Mojo*. https://www.boxofficemojo.com/year/2017/ (accessed January 30, 2023).

5. "Domestic Box Office for 2016," *Box Office Mojo*. https://www.boxofficemojo.com/year/2016/ (accessed January 30, 2023).

2.

On Lasting

"Tradition refuses to submit to the small and arrogant oligarchy of those who happen to be walking about."

—G. K. Chesterton

In the opening chapter, I discussed two kinds of films: classic films, which last, and blockbusters, which do not. The blockbuster is not merely a kind of film, however, but a state of being. Once we understand what blockbuster films, blockbuster novels, and blockbuster albums are, we can identify blockbuster theology and blockbuster ethics, as well.

With very few exceptions, the defining feature of a blockbuster is its ephemerality: it is wildly popular one year and easily replaced by something nearly identical the next year. With even fewer exceptions, the defining feature of a classic is its stability: classics are old. While some might argue that the defining feature of a classic is its goodness, the stability of a classic means that its goodness has been proven over centuries. The goodness of a classic is not like the goodness of a newly-released book or song, for people in a society plagued by blockbusters are quick to declare that new things which they like are "instant classics."

When a book, building, piece of music, or philosophical idea lasts for hundreds or thousands of years, however, its goodness is not claimed just by one kind of people but by rich and poor, Christian and pagan, Catholic and Protestant, East and West.

Between classics and blockbusters, there exists a third kind of thing: common things, which are neither cancerous like blockbusters nor deathless like classics. If blockbusters are very pleasant and classics are very good, common things are a little pleasant and a little good. The wide middle section of every culture consists of common things. Much of our lives are spent in the relative comfort and familiarity of common things: common foods, common tasks, common clothes, common care for health and hygiene. Common things are not extraordinarily good, just plain good. Common things are mortal things, standard things. They do not flatter our senses, but neither do they repay deep contemplation. *The Hobbit* is a common book. *Nebraska* is a common album. Beer is a common beverage. Enchiladas are a common food. Blue jeans are common clothing. Norman Rockwell is a common painter. *The Office* is a common show. Wednesday is a common day. The weather is a common topic. Shoveling the driveway is a common task. A birthday calls for a common celebration.

Different Kinds of Lasting

Whether something is or is not ephemeral can only be proven with time, for the word "ephemeral" refers to things which only exist briefly. In referring to cultural artifacts like movies and songs as ephemeral, I acknowledge that I am stretching the definition of the term, for although Bobby Brown's *Don't Be Cruel* and Tim Burton's *Batman* are far less popular today than when they came out in 1989, they both technically still exist. When I say that many cultural artifacts don't last, I am referring not to their physical qualities but to their spiritual ones: they don't last in the human heart.

Suppose a man paints a picture of a tree in his backyard, frames the painting, and hangs it on the wall in his study. The painting is one of a dozen different decorations in the study, but the man rarely uses his study and neither do his three children. His children come of age and strike out on their own and when the man dies fifty years later, his children pack up his things. None of them is particularly fond of the painted tree, for it did not hang in a prominent place in the home and the children never observed their father gaze at the painting with satisfaction. Nonetheless, they all feel embarrassed to throw away something their father made by hand, even though it means little to them. And so the oldest son puts the painting in a box marked "Dad's Things" and puts the box in his own attic. Fifty years later, the oldest son dies and his children begin dividing up his possessions. They have known for many years that a few boxes of their grandfather's belongings were stored in the attic, but they were never particularly close to their grandfather and so they never felt the need to investigate the contents. Upon the death of their father, however, they sort through their grandfather's things, retain a few valuables, and send the rest off to a charity shop. At the point that the painting of the tree enters the thrift store, it may have lasted more than a hundred years—but only as an object. It has no spiritual or sentimental value, nor does it have any historical significance. The painting never settled deeply into anyone's heart or mind, and so while it exists, no one really knows or cares about it. The man who created it has departed this world, as has any concern for the things he made.

Sentimentalists will find the story of the tree painting sad, but ultimately a person understands that there are too many things in the world to care equally about them all. The sheer volume of things which accrue not only in our present lives but across history demands that we have hierarchical standards by which to judge their value, or else we are condemned to give our lives over entirely to whatever is nearest, easiest, and most accessible. The fact that most things do not last testifies not only to the transitory nature of our world but also to the incomprehensible amount of stuff which not only fills it but would overrun and ultimately destroy it were we not willing to admit just how few things really matter.

Prudence and Consumption

We know from experience that not every cultural artifact which enjoys wild popularity upon its initial release is summarily abandoned by the following year, for more than forty years after making their respective debuts, *Star Wars* and *Dark Side of the Moon* are still wildly popular. Accordingly, situated between works of art which last for centuries (like John Milton's *Paradise Lost* or the *St. Matthew Passion* by Bach) and works of art which quickly come and go, there is a third kind: art which lasts a lifetime, but usually not much longer.

Upon seeing the trailer for the original *Star Wars* film, anyone could have been forgiven for supposing it would prove yet another special effects affair that did well in the box office on opening weekend and then quickly waned in popularity. And yet, it has stuck around. I do not believe that watching *Star Wars* is a waste of time—I think it a fine and prudent way of spending two hours of one's life. Consider, though, that there is nothing about the *Star Wars* trailer which suggests it would be anything other than a typical short-lived blockbuster. Thus, if someone were to see (on opening weekend) every sci-fi film that was released in a year and to justify such use of their time on the grounds that each film might be surprisingly good, such a person would needlessly squander many hundreds of hours, even though the claim that "*The Scorpion King* might be another *Star Wars*" is technically true.

Every new movie "might be the next *Star Wars*," every novel "could be the next *Brave New World*," and every new rock album "could be the next *Dark Side of the Moon*," but recent history and the law of averages teach us that very few movies last as long as *Star Wars*. Even if two hundred magnificent films were released in the United States every year, any man with dignity and common sense (and a job, a family, and a reading life, not to mention commitments to his church, his friends, and his parents) could not make time to see one in ten, and even one in ten would necessitate forsaking all the great movies which came out the previous year, the year before that, and so forth. The rather obvious solution to the problem of not knowing whether a lately released film will be as good as *Star Wars* (or not knowing whether a lately released novel will be as good as *Brave New World*) is to wait twenty years and see if people still think it worth seeing, although this solution requires that a man be willing to not be fashionable and up-to-date.

Because most people intuit the profound ephemerality of popular things, advertisers must either make premature boasts about an item's longevity—i.e. a film or novel that is an "instant classic" or a pair of pants that is "the last pair of khakis you'll ever need"—or else the thing itself must be far more sensual, spectacular, sexy, outrageous, hilarious, cool, or clever than all the popular things which have come before. If a certain cultural artifact is more spectacular, outrageous, or sexy than any other thing of its kind, people will forget that such things tend to not last. The average budget of a blockbuster film gets a little higher every few years, along with the amount of action and violence. In the 1970s and 1980s, special effects adorned films as earrings and a necklace adorn a woman's body; by the 2000s and 2010s, special effects constituted the majority of many films' total running time.

The trajectory of the blockbuster can be seen in other areas of American culture as well. The same sexually explicit lyrics which earned obscenity charges for the Miami rap group 2 Live Crew in 1990 became as common as daisies just twenty years later. During this same time period, the word "extreme" became a fixture in the marketing of new foods—extreme chips, extreme sandwiches, extreme pizza, extreme beer—and each presidential election was sold as the most important one ever, with the advertisements more dire than those of the previous election, the insults traded between candidates more brazen and vile, and campaign budgets expanding toward the infinite.

One could go on indefinitely cataloging all the things in American society which, over the last century, have gradually but constantly veered toward extremity, immoderation, hyper-sensuality, radicalization, and fanaticism. Food, film, politics, and art are easy examples, but we may also include dialogue about health and child-rearing, automobile design, video games, environmental ethics, the identification of mental illnesses, the destigmatization of sexual oddities, the glorification of sports, and the modification of the human body. Everything must be blockbustered.

A Brief Digression to Adjust Terms

Have said this, it will not do to put the word "blockbuster" in front of every noun (i.e. "blockbuster clothes," "blockbuster philosophies") because many of the things which subscribe to blockbuster logic are never terribly popular. Thus, while the term has been serviceable up until this point, I would like to leave "blockbuster" behind and suggest a different word to describe all the spectacular, highly sensual, fashionable, and easily disposable cultural artifacts which partake of the same cup as blockbuster films. The term I prefer is *mediocre*.

Similarly, so far as a discussion of things which last is concerned, the word "classic" will not do because the term is already used too frequently and vaguely. Classic rock stations play music which is less than fifty years old, and classic cars only need to be twenty years old. Even films are speedily declared to be classics—as a testament to just how ephemeral and flimsy most American popular culture is, the Library of Congress is willing to declare a film "culturally, historically, or aesthetically significant" [1] and to add it to the American Film Registry after just ten years. The registry includes everything from *Airplane!* to *Schindler's List*.

Neither will it do to refer to things which last as "high culture." While Beethoven, Dante, and Milton warrant the designation, we must necessarily consider a variety of other lasting things such as Christmas, folktales, and the Nicene Creed which don't fit this category.

The term I prefer for things which last is *uncommon*. I choose it not only because it highlights the rarity of transcendence, but also because it bears a linguistic reference to the word *common*, the term I prefer for average, normal things. Common things and uncommon things are not at odds but are more like friends or lovers; they pour in and out of one another.

To sum up, all cultural artifacts can be parsed out into three categories: *uncommon things, common things,* and *mediocre things.* Mediocre things do not last very long, common things last a lifetime, and uncommon things last indefinitely.

On Mediocrity

Granted, *mediocre* might seem a strange word to describe the flashy, sexy, wildly popular things that we line up at midnight to purchase or stream. Dull, boring, or insipid things are often described as mediocre, along with things that are barely passable or uninspired. A coffee snob might refer to a Starbucks Americano as a "mediocre cup of coffee," for instance. Nearly everyone who has purchased a sandwich at a gas station has thought, "This is mediocre," after taking a bite. For the purposes of this conversation, however, the Starbucks Americano and the gas station sandwich are not *mediocre* but *common*: neither product offers intense sensual pleasure, neither product has been marketed as something people must have right now, and neither product is apt to destroy a desire for classic things, holy things, or works of high culture.

Despite the apparent gap between the conventional use of

"mediocre" (low quality, uninspired) and the particular way in which I am using the word, there is significant overlap. Both uses of "mediocre" suggest something that is dull and boring, with little to no spiritual significance. While a blockbuster film rarely seems dull and boring when it is released, most of them do not age well and strike us later on as pathetic or unnecessary when compared with the even more sensual and outrageous films which replace them. It is my contention that these films—and all mediocre things, for that matter—are actually dull when they are released, but that this dullness is masked by their novelty and our own desire to be fashionable, current, and up-to-date.

Mediocre things appeal to our animal appetites rather than to our spiritual appetites, and thus they are typically sold as things we crave, things we cannot live without, and things we must have right now. Michael Bay makes mediocre movies. E. L. James writes mediocre books. Taco Bell sells mediocre food. H&M sells mediocre clothes. It nearly pains me to offer these specific examples, for mediocre things are so short-lived that mentioning them practically guarantees that this book will have a short shelf life. Ten years after its publication, someone who debates purchasing this book will take it in hand, flip through the pages, see the names Michael Bay and E. L. James, and assume that Joshua Gibbs is also hopelessly obsolete.

Mediocre things offer much more pleasure than common or uncommon things, but this pleasure is short-lived and tends to corrupt our ability to enjoy the uncommon. Mediocre things are not traditional, holy, or natural. We buy them on impulse, enjoy them briefly, and then give them away. Mediocre things may be difficult to diagnose as mediocre when they are on sale, but they seem chintzy, poorly constructed, and stupid just a few years later. Every Goodwill and Salvation Army in this country is awash with DVDs, books, and compact discs that people stayed up until midnight to purchase just a few years ago but which quickly proved to be soulless and silly. Examine a list of the twenty best-selling DVDs and books from just ten years ago and then chart their popularity today: most fall between one thousand and twenty thousand on Amazon's best-seller list. And the films and books which presently occupy the top twenty spots? They're the ones which will clutter the cultural slag heap ten years from now.

Of course, if we look beyond the top twenty spots on Amazon's best-seller list, we find a few older works, a few classics. Depending on the week, half a dozen classics might pepper a list of the one hundred best-selling books in the country. Uncommon things do not offer heart-stopping thrills, and so they do not inspire sudden, rabid interest. They tend to sell steadily, moderately.

Choices

Because our interest in uncommon things is not sudden and passionate, neither is it easily replaced. Unlike *The Da Vinci Code*, copies of Plato's *Gorgias* rarely appear on Goodwill shelves. Few people get rid of *Gorgias* simply because they have read it: reading *Gorgias* once is like taking a single swipe at an old-growth redwood with an axe, and so committing to the book means committing to a half-dozen reads. On the other hand, the difference between a first and second reading of *The Da Vinci Code* is probably a good bit like the difference between the first and second hearings of a joke.

Very few Americans are actually flummoxed over the choice between *Gorgias* and *The Da Vinci Code*, though. The man who reads one of these titles has no interest in reading the other. A consumerist society rarely asks us to choose between an uncommon thing and a mediocre thing. "What shall I listen to this morning—Bach or Drake? What should I do for lunch—make beef bourguignon or get something from KFC? What shall I read this evening—the Epistle of St. James or E. L. James?" These are not real dilemmas that any reasonable person regularly faces. The most persistent dilemma is to choose between a common thing and a mediocre thing.

The most frequently used word in the marketing of mediocre foods is "crave." Mediocre foods are ones that people suddenly and desperately want. The need to fulfill this type of desire is why many fast-food restaurants stay open all night, satisfying customers who saw a commercial at two in the morning during a rerun of a competitive dating show. Likewise, prior to the era of streaming, record stores stayed open until midnight to sell the latest albums by Eminem and Britney Spears. Until quite recently, many movie theaters stayed open until midnight to play the latest installment of a comic book franchise. However, there has never been a midnight premiere for a movie wherein Anthony Hopkins wears a top hat, and restaurants which stay open all night are not selling a lot of buttered peas or green salads after midnight. The creators of gleefully ephemeral things have no respect for time, and thus mediocre things are not meant to be enjoyed at a proper time of day. There is no right or wrong time to consume something which was made to be obsolete in twelve months. It must be enjoyed soon, now, quickly, before our interest in it dries up. The desire for mediocre things is not governed by reason, which is why mediocre things are the ones which are sold in the dead of night through the window of your car. The purchase of a fast food chalupa can bear an eerie resemblance to a purchase made from a drug dealer.

In terms of cost, there is little to no difference between common and mediocre things. One can purchase *The Picture of Dorian Gray* at a bookstore for around the same price as *Fifty Shades of Gray* or *The Da Vinci Code*. For about five dollars, a man can prepare himself a workman's lunch of chips, an apple, and a ham sandwich or he can eat chalupas. It takes no more than five minutes to make a brown bag lunch, but neither does it take more than five minutes to go through the Taco Bell drive-through.

Let us imagine that the man who is deciding between a ham sandwich and chalupas works in construction and moves heavy things all day. It is toilsome, back-breaking labor, and so, unlike other men his age who have sedentary desk jobs, his body has not become pudged with thickness: he has a lean neck, no jowls, and only a little gut. He has not given up, he has not gone to seed, and should he choose to eat chalupas for lunch every day, neither his bathroom scale nor his bank account would really know the difference. What reason has this fellow to make a ham sandwich for lunch?

I pose the question honestly, not rhetorically, because it must be admitted that chalupas are tastier than a ham sandwich. The chalupas offer far more pleasure. They are saltier, fattier, crunchier, and creamier than the sandwich. Everything about the chalupa has been scientifically calculated to please. It is the children's menu re-imagined as the adult's menu; it coddles the palate like a mother coddles a newborn child. But what becomes of the person who accepts being coddled, flattered, and pampered without a second thought? What would a person have to believe about happiness and goodness in order to reject a life of sensual flattery? And why choose things which last when they are not nearly as pleasurable as vapid, ephemeral things?

Endnotes

1. "Selections from the National Film Registry," *Library of Congress*. https://www.loc.gov/collections/selections-from-the-national-film-registry/about-this-collection/ (accessed June 1, 2020).

3.

Uncommon Things

"If their purpose or activity is of human origin, it will fail. But if it is from God, you will not be able to stop these men."

— Acts 5:38–39

I will acknowledge that *uncommon, common,* and *mediocre* are broad and unusual categories to use in the investigation of cultural artifacts and institutions. When writing about culture, every author has to decide how to define the borders of his particular topic. Some historians write books about subjects (music, painting, politics, and so forth) while others write books about historical periods (the late antique, the medieval, the Renaissance). An art critic might narrow in on a single genre within a larger art form (jazz, still life paintings, the epic poem, the requiem mass) or decide to group artists by country or religion (English, French, Christian, Buddhist). What I intend to write, however, is a sort of existential history book, the premise of which is that the fact that Mozart's *Requiem in D Minor* (an eighteenth-century Austrian mass), the Chartres Cathedral (a thirteenth-century French Christian church), the

Odyssey (an eighth-century BC Greek pagan poem), Christmas (a second-century Roman Christian holiday), *Narrative of the Life of Frederick Douglass* (a nineteenth-century American autobiography), *One Thousand and One Nights* (a medieval Muslim anthology of short fiction), and Artemisia Gentileschi's *Judith Slaying Holofernes* (a seventeenth-century Italian painting) have all lasted makes them similar enough to be considered as a single subject.

As a justification for considering all of these things to be of a kind, I would ask readers to reflect on the relatively small number of things which last.

Take a wide survey of all the objects in your home and ask yourself how many will last a hundred years. Of course, clocks will still be around one century from now, but not the clock presently hanging on your wall. All the bottles, bookends, board games, cribs, coats, crockpots, plates, pots, pans, purses, pens, and pillows will be gone in a hundred years, and the same is true of a thousand other objects in your home and in one billion other homes around the world.

Objects are not alone in their impermanence: the memory of other human beings fades rather quickly, as well. Every human being has four grandparents, eight great-grandparents, sixteen great-great-grandparents, and so forth, but few people can name more than one or two of their great-grandparents and fewer still know any important details about their lives. We do not know the labors to which they committed their lives. We do not know their beliefs, their greatest failures, or their successes. We have not read any of their letters, curiously turned their jewelry over in our fingers, studied photographs of their faces, or visited their graves to lay flowers. Some might argue that this for-getfulness comes because most people spend so little time with their great-grandparents; however, if a man is largely ignorant of his great-grandparents, it generally means that his mother and father rarely remembered their grandparents out loud. Unless they lived uncommonly glorious lives, a man does not regularly have a need to speak of his own grandparents. Thus, the average man is forgetful of his great-grandparents and his children will be the same way.

Next to objects and memories, emotions are even more transient. The teenage heartbreak that I once swore would cast a shadow over my entire life now strikes me as merely comic. I have seen students torn apart in the morning by news that one of their classmates died during the night; a black cloud hangs over the remainder of the school day, but by the time dismissal rolls around, they are laughing and joking merrily. Resolutions, oaths, and companies do not last: every generation confesses fresh surprise that their grandparents' favorite store has lately gone bankrupt, even though very few stores exceed the average human lifespan. Ethics and morals do not last, for what was considered enlightened and generous twenty years ago is thought racist, sexist, or bigoted today. Grudges, loves, and friendships do not last. Irreplaceable employees are replaced. Widows remarry.

Time devours objects, memories, and emotions, but also movements, art, knowledge, and belief. Worse still, time devours human beings. Man was created to subdue the earth, yet the earth finally subdues every man. *Time devours absolutely everything. Nothing survives. Nothing lasts...*

And yet—quite miraculously—a few things do actually last.

Against the reliability of common sense, the laws of science, the ravages of sin, the tendencies of mankind, and the meta-physics which govern creation, some things are not destroyed by time. The ability to last is so exceedingly rare that when a man finds something which has bested time, he has found a thing for which there is only one fitting adjective: *divine*. Given that lasting is such a rare quality for anything to have, grouping to-gether all those things which have lasted—regardless of when they were created, what part of the world they hail from, or what creed their creators held to—is no more strange than taking a survey of medieval things, African things, Baroque things, or Muslim things.

How long must a thing last before we say it *has lasted*, though? Very few books have lasted more than two thousand years, but considerably more have lasted a thousand years, more still have lasted five hundred years, and many millions of titles are still available in the decade after they first appear. At what age does a thing's longevity become impressive and strange? As a teacher of old books at a classical school, I often field skeptical questions from students about what it means for something to be old, a relative term. At what point does a thing become a classic? Tra-ditionalists and conservatives often defend those things which have "stood the test of time," but how much time is sufficient to test a thing?

Allow me to offer a simple answer: A thing has stood the test of time if it is still loved, studied, understood, revered, sold, or practiced one hundred years after the death of its creator.

One hundred years is no arbitrary period, though. It is not simply a nice, round number. In his remarkable essay "The Im-possibility of Secular Society," French medieval scholar Rémi Brague writes:

The root of words like secular, secularism, and secularity is saeculum. From this Latin word the Romance languages derived their words for the word century: siècle, secolo, siglo... [A century] is the temporal limit of living memory. It is the halo of possible experience that surrounds the life of the individual. I can keep a remembrance of my grandparents and, more seldom, of my great-grandparents. What my grandfather told me I can tell my grandchildren. I can reach back two generations and forward two, but rarely more, to a period spanning what amounts to a century. [1]

Every man is thus constantly caught up in a four-generation span. My grandparents are alive, my parents are alive, I am alive, my children are alive: here are four generations. By the time I have grandchildren, my parents will be on the cusp of death and the four-generation span is preserved. By the time I have great-grandchildren, I will be on the cusp of death and the four-generation span is yet preserved. Given that the age of a generation is twenty-five years, the four-generation span is a period of time which always approximates a century, and thus the century is preserved as a unit of time.

Elsewhere in the essay, Brague also describes the century as the limit of direct care.[2] I may benefit my children and my grandchildren in tangible and concrete ways; however, although I may someday hold my great-grandchildren in my arms, there is little chance that they will remember me when they are grown. Human sentiment is likewise bound to this four-generation limit. For example, if a grown man were to learn that his mother was assaulted when she was a child, he would respond with profound horror and sadness. If he learned that his grandmother was assaulted when a child, he would respond with horror, but probably a good deal less horror than he would upon learning of the assault on his mother. If he learned that his great-grandmother was assaulted as a child, he might not have a particularly visceral reaction. Upon learning that his great-great-grandmother was assaulted as a child, a man's response might not be altogether different from hearing it said that "children have been violently mistreated for centuries." Reasonable people do not weep when they first read of Caesar's death in history books, and although accounts of mistreated slaves in the American South make a man's blood boil, he is not so much angry with the dead slave owners as with their living apologists.

After the creator of a cultural artifact (symphony, painting, book, building, and so forth) has been dead for one hundred years, we may know with certainty that no living person has been directly benefited by the creator. No one alive ever met him, spoke with him, or stood on planet earth at the same time, breathing the same air as he did. A hundred years after a man's death, natural human affection for him has dried up and he is nothing more than an abstraction, an idea. No one carries a torch for his memory, describes the love they received from him, or champions the spirit they have inherited from him. If people are still willing to listen to a man one hundred years after his death, he speaks from the grave. No one alive who yet cares for him has any natural reason for doing so, and after natural affection passes, if any affection remains, it is supernatural.

On the Soul

The growing power and presence of mediocrity in American

culture depends largely on materialist principles which were popularized by Enlightenment philosophers and codified by French Revolutionaries. Later chapters will contemplate both the Enlightenment and the French Revolution, but suffice it to say for now that if mediocrity is a state of being, a more general discussion of being is necessary in order to understand good and bad art.

While it is fashionable in a secularist society to talk about art as a spiritual or psychic enterprise, speaking coherently about what exactly the soul *is* requires study and careful elucidation. Speaking incoherently about the soul is relatively easy, though, and thus it is a popular and lucrative modern pastime. The soul is no longer thought of as a particular thing, like the liver or the heart, but as a way of talking about what we want and how we feel. Modern men take it for granted that advice about care for the liver or the heart should only come from people who have extensively studied these organs, proven the profundity of their knowledge to panels of seasoned experts, and confirmed their expertise by a long track record of having healed people and saved lives. If a person with no medical training sells advice on medical care, he can be regarded as a fraud, sued, fined, or sent to jail.

On the other hand, modern people are willing to accept all kinds of unproven, experimental advice on curing the ills of the soul. This advice comes from a number of places: motivational speakers, inspirational meme pages, Instagram influencers, political idealists, screenwriters of fantasy films, and celebrity pastors, all of whom regularly speak on the subject of the soul even though few of them could answer rather mundane questions about it, like what the soul is, where it is, whether it is immortal, and so forth. Given how unconcerned secularists are about these questions, their occasional references to the soul hardly constitute real belief in its existence.

It might surprise them to learn that, much like statecraft, Trinitarian theology, animal husbandry, and geometry, the soul has been the subject of robust academic interest for thousands of years. In the last three thousand years, philosophers have proven as much about the soul as geologists have proven about plate tectonics, although knowledge of the soul is far more stable than knowledge about the earth. A good deal of what Plato taught about the soul twenty-five centuries ago is still accepted by modern theologians from a host of different religious traditions. To put it bluntly, the soul is no more a mystery than the Mediterranean Sea. The fact that most people cannot speak about it with certainty doesn't mean nobody can, even while much remains unknown.

Since the French Revolution, the relationship between art and the human soul has been trivialized by the idea that art is primarily about self-expression rather than communion with God, the cultivation of virtue, or the redemption of ugliness. Anyone who wants to undertake the difficult task of learning to enjoy good things and who wants to forsake the sensual trash which proliferates in a consumerist society must be willing to consider the relationship between the soul and art, which is food to the soul.

In Aristotle's *Physics*, he argues that the existence of a thing depends on four separate causes: the material cause (the substance from which a thing is made), the formal cause (the design or idea imposed upon the substance), the efficient cause (the person or process which conceives of the design), and the final cause (the purpose of the thing). In other words, the creation of a thing always involves a person impressing an idea upon a substance for a reason. All things thus have both a material and an immaterial aspect, a body and a soul.

In *Nichomachean Ethics*, Aristotle distinguishes three kinds of soul: vegetative soul, sensitive soul, and noetic soul. A vegetative soul is proper to all existing things which are incapable of making decisions, such as plants and trees. A sensitive soul is proper to animals, which are capable of perceiving, deciding, and being trained, but not of speech. While some animals can respond to vocal commands, animals are incapable of discerning a range of meanings from the same sign. A dog might wag its tail happily when it hears the word "walk," but it cannot tell the difference between "walk," a journey, and "wok," the Chinese cooking pot. Animals respond to certain words the way computers respond to the push of certain buttons, and a computer cannot tell when a man has pushed the power button in a state of despair or of joy. A noetic soul is proper only to men and angels, though, for it entails perception and contemplation, the ability to simultaneously consider the past and the future. The unique position of the human soul is that it serves a physical body. Because men have bodies, they die; because men have noetic souls, they contemplate the future. Angels do not contemplate their own deaths because they are immortal, and animals do not contemplate their own deaths because they are not rational beings. Only man contemplates his own death.

All of this matters to a discussion of art because every artist impresses his own noetic soul upon a substance of some kind, like canvas, paper, paint, stone, strings, marble, and so forth. Every substance is ephemeral and destructible, but the soul is eternal—thus, when the artist impresses his soul into a substance, the substance retains some properties of the soul. If the soul is impressed deeply enough, the substance may retain the soul's eternality.

Creating any sort of cultural artifact entails impressing soul onto substance, even if not all cultural artifacts require the same unique and expressive soul of a painter or composer. For example, let us imagine two tables, one made by a novice and the other made by a master carpenter. Both tables are made of the same substance: wood and screws. The form of either table is basically the same: a broad, shallow top and four legs. Of these two tables, the better table is the one which retains the form of a table for longer. The inferior table may lose its form in one of two ways. First, the table may be not be able sustain much use and collapse the first time someone places a Thanksgiving turkey on top of it. Second, the table may be very ugly and thus the owner tires of it quickly, takes it apart, and turns it into other things. The table which lasts will both serve its purpose and inspire its owners to properly care for it, thereby increasing its lifespan. If the table is beautiful, the owner will be more likely to preserve it and repair it. It is unlikely that the novice carpenter has the depth and generosity of soul necessary to deeply impress the form into the substance.

The inferior table quickly loses its form because the maker did not deeply impress the table soul into the table substance. This is true even if the inferior table is sturdy, for if it has no beauty, the owner is not likely to feel much loyalty to it and will not hesitate to get rid of it when he is able to afford a new one. There are millions of cheap card tables in this country (the gray metal sort with folding legs), and no matter how long one such table lasts, no one feels bad about throwing it away when something better comes along.

What is true of two tables is true of books, music, poems, cathedrals, and holidays, as well. Nikolai Gogol's "The Mysterious Portrait" tells the story of a Tchartkoff, a poor but talented young painter who suddenly comes upon a windfall of money, buys himself some good press, and begins painting portraits of aristocrats' children. Tchartkoff flatters the aristocrats, though, and makes their haughty children appear more fair and dignified than they truly are. His portraits remove moles and blemishes, make noses smaller and more narrow, and feign nobility on the brows of cowards. Year by year, Tchartkoff loses his talent and eventually his interest in painting, even as his celebrity grows. Some time after establishing himself as a socialite and critic, he is asked to judge an art contest. When Tchartkoff arrives at the gallery where the paintings are to be judged, he finds a crowd gathered around one canvas. Of the painting that the crowd gazes at, Gogol writes:

> *All seemed united in it: the art of Raphael, reflected in the lofty grace of the grouping; the art of Correggio, breathing from the finished perfection of the workmanship. But more striking than all else was the evident creative power in the artist's mind. The very minutest object in the picture revealed it; he had caught that melting roundness of outline which is visible in nature only to the artist creator, and which comes out as angles with a copyist. It was plainly visible how the artist, having imbibed it all from the external world, had first stored it in his mind, and then drawn it thence, as from a spiritual source, into one harmonious, triumphant song.*

And it was evident, even to the uninitiated, how vast a gulf there was fixed between creation and a mere copy from nature. Involuntary tears stood ready to fall in the eyes of those who surrounded the picture. It seemed as though all joined in a silent hymn to the divine work.[3]

The copyist (or hyperrealist) is really a materialist who is incapable of perceiving the souls of things. The artist, on the other hand, takes in the world as a bee takes in nectar. What the artist creates, though, is not just the world, but the world glorified. The artist does not see the world accurately, but rightly—not factually, but truthfully. In storing the world within his own spirit, the artist purges it of all that is ephemeral and passing. When the world is brought forth again, it is eternal. In *Why Beauty Matters*, Sir Roger Scruton argues, "The skill of the true artist is to show the real in the light of the ideal and so transfigure it."[4] The copyist and the hyperrealist magnify the suffering and volatility of the world, but the artist redeems it.

Christian Contempt for Uncommon Things

To participate in any cultural artifact or institution, then—to listen to music, to read a book, to sing a hymn in a cathedral nave, to drink a glass of wine—is to partake of both a soul and a substance. Every made thing offers the real presence of its maker. In the same way that Christians should not say to the poor, "Go in peace; be warmed and filled," and pretend they have done their duty, neither should they be content with mere analysis of a work of art.

Christians are poorly positioned to understand the spiritual aspects of art, however, because of their belief in the importance of message. Moral absolutism has made Christians shallow, although they could not have predicted such dire consequences in the 1980s and 1990s. When the spirit of our age inclined sharply toward moral relativism, conservative Christians rejected the zeitgeist in favor of the idea that every thought, word, and deed was either right or wrong, good or evil, and that these categories were absolute and objective. Worldview analysis emerged as an important hermeneutic during this time. However, because worldview analysis tends to be conducted by moral absolutists, it is not so much a hermeneutic as an anti-hermeneutic, a rejection of interpretive strategies: all cultural artifacts are either good or bad, right or wrong. The worldview analyst thus conceives of a consistently violent role for the reader or viewer, who must tear off the illusory husk of the story or the painting and get to the kernel of belief within.

Despite such verve and passion for truth, the Christian brand is now rightly denigrated as trite and trivial. To put the word "Christian" before a children's book, song, or work of art is to give the assumption that it tends toward cut-rate design and cheap sentimentality. One has a far better chance of finding the works of Aquinas and Augustine at Barnes & Noble than at a Christian bookstore, for Christian bookstores traffic primarily in books that are not very old and will not be read for many years in the future. Christian tradition has long venerated Truth, Beauty, and Goodness as the three transcendent revelations of God, and yet in fighting moral relativism, American Christians largely abandoned any interest in Beauty and Goodness and doubled down on Truth. Our residual fear of "works righteousness" is nothing more than a fear of righteous works, a sad byproduct of our exclusive interest in abstract, unembodied Truth. Where Beauty does not matter, Goodness usually does not either.

It is this unbalanced, imprudent, and exaggerated fixation on Truth which led Christians into an obsession with the "good message." We do not care what kind of zany, silly antics a television program inspires in our children provided the show teaches that "stealing is wrong." Christian films are typically stocked with cardboard characters and implausible, preachy dialog, yet Christians come away praising such stories for explicitly teaching that adultery is wrong or that we should not lose hope. We are content that a minister of the gospel could preach a sermon while wearing a clown suit provided that he spoke to children about the value of sharing, obeying your parents, or some other ready platitude. While worldview analysis is no longer fashionable and a sycophantically lenient hermeneutic has taken its place, the Christian obsession with message remains.

The commercial success of the Christian film *Fireproof* (2008) makes for a convenient example of message-oriented art. The film tells the story of Caleb and Catherine Holt, a selfish couple in a failing and childless marriage, who jointly reimagine their marriage in terms of sacrifice. Upon recognizing he is on the cusp of divorce, Caleb accepts the advice of his father to wholeheartedly give himself to his wife for forty days, caring nothing for his own comfort, to see if this renewed devotion could save his marriage. It could. What is more, both Caleb and Catherine become Christians as a result of their decision to save their marriage. Naturally, the forty-day program of selfless devotion is described in a book which the husband reads, and the book is, in fact, also a product which viewers of the film can purchase when the film is over. The book is entitled *The Love Dare*, and to date, it has sold well north of three million copies. The film might simply be an infomercial for the book, but this seems overly cynical. Considered apart from its advertising qualities, the message of *Fireproof* is unambiguous and hardly requires a single viewing to discern, let alone repeat viewings: a Christian marriage is a selfless marriage and only selfless marriages thrive.

The problem with a good message is that it does not last. Nothing is more forgettable than a good message. The message of *Fireproof* is obviously true, and no reasonable Christian would have any interest in denying or disputing the matter. The message is also not without power: after watching the film, I was more mindful around the house. I washed the dishes more often, put a few extra loads of laundry through the washer, made a greater effort to listen attentively when my wife spoke. Spending two hours watching a man with a lousy marriage struggle to perform works of charity, mercy, and hope is good for the soul, regardless of the miserable artistic value. This is the power of an image. A man becomes what he beholds.

However, the effect of watching *Fireproof* only lingered for a few days, and then I returned to my old self. A smoker might see an anti-smoking commercial wherein a few images of black lungs and surgically-implanted throat microphones are flashed on the screen, and such images might prevent the man from lighting up for half an hour. However, they are not likely to persuade him to quit forever. So, too, *Fireproof* offers a few unnerving images, but the story is not a deep reflection on marriage. The couple's problems are not revealed via scenes filled with careful, minute observations on the subtle ways in which husbands and wives come to ignore, revile, disgust, and disappoint one another. While talking with friends, Caleb complains, "Then [my wife] starts nagging

me and saying that I don't listen to her . . . or something like
that." Such lines suggest the filmmakers have as little interest
in the difficulties of marriage as Caleb has in the difficulties of
his wife's life. In another scene, Caleb phones his father and begins the conversation with, "I think Catherine and I are done. .
. . No, it's over. She wants out." Between the claim that he and
Catherine "are done" and the corrective, "No, it's over," there is
perhaps half a second. What objection is his father able to make
in that little eyelash of a pause? The fact that the pause is not
long enough for his father to say anything is not a concern of the
filmmakers. It is a token pause.

Neither are the filmmakers concerned with the fact that most
men are loath to talk about marriage problems and even more
loath to speak with their fathers about them. The remainder
of the film shows that Caleb does not have a strong relationship with his father to begin with, which makes it all the more
unbelievable that he would call him and immediately divulge a
highly personal and embarrassing piece of information. What
is more, the makers of *Fireproof* do not seem to understand the
nature of men, women, or even the personalities of their own
characters. Caleb's conversation with his father is a token conversation, discussing the token problems of a token marriage in
what ultimately proves a token movie about a token human institution. The characters' problems are writ sufficiently large that
not a soul could miss them or misunderstand them. Less than
ten minutes into the film, the couple articulately explains their
gripes to one another, and at no point throughout the remainder
of film are these gripes complicated or deepened with further
revelation.

Likewise, after watching *Fireproof*, I performed a token washing of the dishes, a token load of laundry, and when my desire to be a better husband faded several days later, I felt no compulsion to go back and watch the movie again, because the movie could ultimately be reduced to a single message which I could still recall clearly. The message of the film was fine, but fine messages alone do not transform people. Had there been something beautiful and poignant about the story, I might have gone back to watch it again and again, thereby internalizing the film over a period of years. But in and of itself, a good message is rarely enough to transform the hearer.

Christ describes this in the parable of the sower:

> A sower went out to sow. And as he sowed, some seeds fell along the path, and the birds came and devoured them. Other seeds fell on rocky ground, where they did not have much soil, and immediately they sprang up, since they had no depth of soil, but when the sun rose they were scorched. And since they had no root, they withered away. Other seeds fell among thorns, and the thorns grew up and choked them. Other seeds fell on good soil and produced grain, some a hundredfold, some sixty, some thirty. He who has ears, let him hear. (Matt 13:3-9, ESV)

Christ later tells the apostles that the seed represents "the word of the kingdom" and that the soil represents the hearts of those who hear the word. The seed does not transform the soil. Rather, some hearts are capable of receiving the word and others are not. Receiving the word of the kingdom requires preparation, which is why Jesus Christ did not appear on Earth unannounced. Instead, John the Baptist came first and taught people how to prepare themselves for the Messiah. John's message was one of charity, honesty, and sacrifice: "Whoever has two tunics is to share with him who has none, and whoever has food is to do likewise ... Collect no more than you are authorized to do ... Be content with your wages" (Luke 3:11,13,14). These are not works which save a man. Rather, these are works which enlarge and deepen the soul so that the soul can receive the word of the kingdom. John's preparatory teaching coincides with Christ's interpretation of the parable of the sower, for the thorns which choke the word are "the worries of this life and the deceitfulness of wealth" (Mark 4:19).

The man who only ever exposes himself to good messages issued from shallow spirits is more likely to adopt that shallowness of spirit than the goodness of the message. For this reason, a man's soul might gain more in reading the *Aeneid* than another Christian book about the family, for nothing is more disposable than Christian books about the family. The Christian husband who reads a pop theology book about the family might be extra nice to his wife for the two weeks after he finishes it but become a more shallow person in the long run. As the parable of the sower teaches, shallow soil produces quickly, but the productivity does not last.

Having taught classical literature at Christian schools for many years, I occasionally speak with parents who are concerned that their sons and daughters are reading pagan literature. Other parents cut to the chase and ask of *Jane Eyre* or *Hamlet*, "What is the message of this story?" While *Jane Eyre* does not lack a good message, reducing the book to a message is like calculating the number of calories in Christmas dinner and then serving everyone in the family eight warm ounces of canola oil and a couple multivitamins because it was cheaper and faster than serving prime rib, scalloped potatoes, blue cheese, asparagus and a 2009 Châteauneuf-du-Pape. Indeed, it would be cheaper and faster—but what would all the time and money saved be spent on instead?

Uncommon Contentment

As can be seen in John the Baptist's teachings about preparing for the Messiah's arrival, enlarging the soul is not always enjoyable, for it usually involves depriving the body of some festal thing. While feasting can enlarge the soul, feasting is only true feasting when it completes a fast. The man who feasts without ceasing is simply a glutton. Because American Christians love feasting, celebration, encouragement, and grace, they tend to have little interest in the penitential practices which make feasting and celebration safe. We have even become so disgusted by mourning that we turn funerals into occasions of celebration and jocularity.

Similarly, evangelical Christians talk quite a bit about the salvation of souls but have very little else to say about them. Because most American Christians conceive of salvation primarily as a judicial decision in their favor, the question of what souls should do after they are saved is rather baffling. It is no wonder modern Christians struggle to make lasting art, let alone appreciate all the beautiful art their forebears made which has lasted. The lastingness of art is a spiritual consideration that does not directly pertain to salvation.

While the Baptist prescribes giving away food and clothing and refraining from theft, he also teaches his hearers to "be content," which is a far more abstract instruction. The point of mediocre art is to inflame desire and destroy contentment because content people buy less. Good art is bad for business.

Uncommon things have an entirely different economy than carnal things, however, and the man who has a taste for uncommon things and avoids mediocrity leads a life of contentment. When it comes to purely carnal things, like potato chips or pornography, more leads to more. Pleasure takes place in the body but satisfaction is of the soul, and so things which offer purely physical pleasure cannot help egging people on to consume more and more in search of a spiritual state which the carnal thing is incapable of delivering. The economy of spiritual things is not like this, however, because spirit is immaterial, intellectual, and unquantifiable. There is not "more Christ" in a large bite of the Eucharist than a small one; neither is the object blessed with a bucket of holy water more holy than an object blessed with a thimbleful. Inasmuch as a thing appeals more to the spirit than the body, a man needs less of it: while many people have accidentally eaten an entire bag of Doritos in one sitting, no one has ever accidentally read the entire Gospel of St. John in one sitting.

While some preachers are given to comparing the amount of time parishioners spend watching television to the amount of time they spend reading their Bibles, it is God Himself who first lays out rather lopsided proportions for our secular and sacred needs: for every six common days, there is one uncommon day. This does not mean that the needs of the body are more important than the needs of the spirit, for Christ teaches the opposite during His earthly ministry. He tells His followers not to fear those who can "destroy the body" but He who can "throw body and soul into Hell" (Matt. 10:28). When the paralytic is lowered through the roof, Christ heals his soul first—only after the man's sins are forgiven does Christ restore his body. As such, the fact that sacred things are given a smaller portion of the week than secular things suggests the two cannot be measured on the same scale. God can do more for the soul in one day than He can do for the body in six. Thus, the man who invests in spiritual things necessarily gets a better return than the man who invests in carnal things, where "moth and rust destroy and where thieves break in and steal" (Matt. 6:19). The more a man experiences spiritual satisfaction, the less interested he is in purely carnal things.

Several years ago, for Lent, I vowed to only listen to music which was composed more than one hundred years ago. As the penitential season progressed, I found I was simply listening to less music. There is nothing strange about finishing one Coldplay album and immediately putting in another (at least, not for the person who likes the band enough to listen to an entire album), but one cannot do so with Beethoven's symphonies without feeling gluttonous. Very good things exhaust the senses through the mind, while mediocre things pummel the senses without ever reaching the mind. The spirit can be satisfied but "the eye is not satisfied with seeing, nor the ear filled with hearing" (Eccl. 1:8), which is why we binge-watch sexy, funny, thrilling TV shows and stage mediocre movie marathons, but we are always content with just one movie wherein Anthony Hopkins wears a top hat.

When the lately liberated Israelites longed for the bondage of Egypt, it was not the quality of Egyptian food they missed but the quantity: "If only we had died by the Lord's hand in Egypt! There we sat around pots of meat and ate all the food we wanted" (Exod. 16:3). This is epitomized by the buffet restaurant which caters to people who are enslaved to their desires by advertising all-you-can-eat meals. Such a business assumes that patrons sit down to eat with the mentality of a looter who cannot help being frustrated that he only has two arms with which to steal and one home in which to store his plunder. Are people who capitalize on the promise of an all-you-can-eat restaurant not ultimately disappointed that *they can only eat so much?* If a man stops eating merely because he cannot eat any more, he does not leave the restaurant satisfied but defeated.

The rise of the craft food and beverage industry (prior to the 2020 pandemic, at least) led most of the middle class to view the all-you-can-eat model as passé and vulgar, but this sentiment did not extend to all-you-can-stream movies, television, music, audiobooks, and so forth. However, it is not difficult to discern that the appeal of music which is popular on an all-you-can-stream platform is not all that different from the appeal of food which is popular on an all-you-can-eat buffet. Thus, while American food was becoming more expensive and selective, many other American cultural enterprises became alarmingly cheap and dangerously plentiful.

Endnotes

1. Remi Brague, "The Impossibility of Secular Society," *First Things*. October 2013, https://www.firstthings.com/article/2013/10/the-impossibility-of-secular-society (accessed June 1, 2020).

2. *Ibid.*

3. Nikolai Gogol, *Taras Bulba and Other Tales*. Project Gutenberg, https://www.gutenberg.org/ebooks/1197 (Accessed June 1, 2020).

4. *Why Beauty Matters*, directed by Louise Lockwood (BBC Two, 2009).

4.

Art As We Know It

"There is hardly anything in the world that some man cannot make a little worse and sell a little cheaper, and the people who consider price only are this man's lawful prey."
                                    —*Attributed to John Ruskin*

There is just something special about art of the twentieth century.

No contemporary book about art can properly address its subject without first saying something about twentieth-century art, which, when placed in the vast history of artistic endeavors, appears in the costume of a clown at a black-tie state dinner. The twentieth century is not a matter to be saved for the last chapter of an art history book, though a chronological arrangement would place it toward the end. Rather, art of the twentieth century will be—for any honest aesthetic theorist—the hitch, the snag, the outlier which skews an otherwise predictable model.

The peculiarity of twentieth-century art is better described not by experts but by the same little boy who critiqued the proverbial emperor's new wardrobe. Some subjects cannot be dealt with honestly by anyone other than an authority, while other

subjects are nearly bereft of honest experts, and I think twentieth-century art is clearly an example of the latter. A good deal
of representative twentieth-century works must be described
honestly and forthrightly by as naïve a man as you can find, the
kind of fellow who is not out to impress anyone with the novelty
or brilliance of his opinions. I think the same thing is also true
of child-rearing and marriage, both subjects for which I would
more readily accept the advice of a tired old provincial crone
than an unpracticed theorist who received his doctorate in the
subject just last week.

When surveying the long history of art, a number of iconic
twentieth-century pieces announce themselves loudly as being
very special. One may observe a great continuity in art prior to
the twentieth century, a continuity which was not immediately
broken by the French Revolution, although the French Revolution planted seeds which would finally bear fruit after the First
World War. The continuity of art prior to this time was not one
of style, for Renaissance and Rococo art are easily distinguished
by someone who has scratched the surface of art history, nor of
subject matter, because the explosion of genres which occurred
in seventeenth-century Holland (for example) could not have
been predicted by painters prior to the Reformation, and yet all
those bowls of fruit make perfect sense when seen in the light of
later Dutch wealth.

What, then, is the continuity of art prior to the twentieth
century?

A common man, i.e. a man with some common sense and
no college education, would likely have difficulty distinguishing
art of the fourteenth century from art of the fifteenth century.
So, too, art of the fifteenth and sixteenth centuries can easily be

confused, as can art of the sixteenth and seventeenth centuries. A certain painting of the crucifixion might believably come from a date between 1500 and 1900. Any blue-collar construction worker from middle America—a beer drinker who admitted he knew nothing about art—could be shown slides of Titian, Fra Angelico, Raphael, Goya, Delacroix, Corot, or Courbet, and not be able to guess within a hundred years either way when each painter made their mark. But the moment our man was shown a painting by Willem de Kooning, Mark Rothko, Franz Kline, or Robert Motherwell, he could wager with dogmatic certainty that it came from none other than the twentieth century. Between the nineteenth and twentieth centuries, something came to a grinding halt.

Iconic, emblematic works of the twentieth century announce their youth with great bombast. Twentieth-century art unambiguously proclaims that the standards and conventions of beauty accepted by all Christian people in bygone eras have been wholeheartedly rejected—not edited and refined, but degraded and discarded. Form was diminished. Image was no longer necessary. Within the context of twentieth-century art, all the subtle differences between styles and genres and epochs vanish. The construction worker knows that Jackson Pollock's *Autumn Rhythm* is from the twentieth century because it does not depict things. Before the twentieth century, styles varied from one era to the next, but painters depicted a recognizable set of subjects: Christ, the saints, aristocrats, animals, laborers gathering in a field, nude women, bowls of fruit, the English countryside, shipwrecks on the beach, the battered remains of cathedrals, arrangements of flowers, scenes from Greek mythology and the Old Testament. By contrast, a good deal of twentieth-century art does not depict these things or *any* things. This is because the difference between twentieth-century art and all that came before it is not merely one of style or preference, but theology.

This is true not only of paintings, but of music and literature as well. After one has heard the music of John Cage, the music of Mozart, Vivaldi, and Debussy all sound like they might be cousins. The American teenager who has been nursed on pop music simply refers to every unfamiliar instrumental tune as "classical music," no matter what era it comes from. It all sounds the same to him. The term is not an insult, nor is it spoken out of ignorance, for even knowledgeable NPR disc jockeys refer to their midday format as "classical." Rather, the term "classical music" offers a fair and practical distinction. "Classical music" is an unwitting concession to the fact that art of the twentieth century never fails to stick out like a sore thumb.

A caveat, though: not every twentieth-century painter is as weird as Kandinsky, not every twentieth-century composer is as pretentious as John Cage, and not every twentieth-century novel is as unreadable as *Gravity's Rainbow*. One could even argue that, taken as a whole, only a relatively small portion of the art created in the twentieth century has much in common with artists like Cage, Kandinsky, and Pynchon. What is more, a small number of twentieth-century artists (Ravel and Rachmaninoff come to mind) created work which might be mistaken for the work of some bygone century in which men respected tradition. But with this caveat, we have the makings of an acrimonious debate.

The Fate of the West

A certain kind of outrage is performed in our time by prim conservatives wherein pearls are clutched with one hand while the other points wildly at the works of the avant-garde—and then the shrill lament goes up, "The West is dying." Progressives commonly dismiss such pearl-clutching by pointing at all the television programs and films from the 1950s and 1960s that preached conventional morality and bland aesthetics, not to mention the robust business which the Hallmark Channel does today, or the fact that country music (which leans heavily Republican) and contemporary Christian record labels make billions of dollars every year. Thus progressives argue that if the West—at least as conservatives see it—was actually dying, bland family-friendly entertainment would be much harder to come by. "Not much has really changed in the last two hundred years," argues the Left. "Conservatives simply overreact every time they have to give a little ground. What was common at the founding of this country is still common today."

Even if you play this game and reduce culture to a set of numbers, plenty of people whose tastes in books and music are conservative (at least on paper) nonetheless use and interpret their books and music in a thoroughly progressive manner. For fifteen years, I have been a teacher at classical Christian schools where most of the students come from families that proudly vote Republican. Nonetheless, the default position most of my students take on matters of art and beauty is entirely atheistic. Atheistic beliefs about art and beauty are so common and so deeply ingrained in the American psyche that most Christians do not know there is any alternative.

Many students take it for granted that all judgments of beauty are relative and that claiming one piece of art is objectively better than another is arrogant at best and probably bigoted as well. Taste is thought to be a matter of personal preference, which means taste cannot be good or bad and thus neither can art. To claim that Frida Kahlo's work is better than Jean-Michel Basquiat's work (or vice versa) is a personal insult to everyone who enjoys Basquiat's work more. The goodness of art entirely comes down to the pleasure and meaning that the audience derives from it. No work of art possesses goodness or brilliance on its own, so both pleasure and meaning originate within the viewer, the listener, or the reader. While some students raised in theologically savvy households have been taught to scoff at such relativistic philosophy, they often hold nonetheless to the progressive belief which ultimately gives birth to all the rest, which is that art is fundamentally an act of self-expression.

Before and After the French Revolution

Before the French Revolution, art had little to do with the self. During the Renaissance, had you asked any man what the point of art was, he would have told you it was beauty, for beauty revealed God Himself. To create something beautiful was to reach up toward heaven, to touch the face of God and to manifest the Divine with paint, stone, word, or song here on Earth. The creation of beautiful art did not involve an inward orientation. Rather, the skill of the artist was simply the height of his reach. Man's interest in beauty lasted in proportion to his belief in God. As his confidence in God diminished, so did his motivation to create beautiful things. What replaced God, of course, was the self.

Older artists did not reach inward because they already knew what they would find—the same things all men find when they reach into their own hearts: selfishness, hostility, frustration, perversion, hatred, and so forth. The man who dipped his brush into his own psyche and flung whatever clung to the bristles onto a canvas could only multiply the ugliness of the world. The visual gibberish of the abstract expressionists was not meant to be an honest account of the transcendent God, but rather the disordered expression of a disordered soul.

Thus far, I have connected the world after the French Revolution with a number of complaints about the twentieth century. Conservative authors so regularly put the bill for modern ills on the French Revolution's tab that a man unfamiliar with modern continental history is justified in asking what exactly happened in 1789 that sent the whole world careening toward chaos— or, if not chaos, at least all those qualities of modern life that conservative intellectuals loathe. A cursory glance at any textbook account of the French Revolution quickly unveils a host of events which any reasonable person, conservative or otherwise, will find horrific. An atheistic mob seizes power, declares itself the rightful government, incites riots, then executes the king and queen. Priests are beheaded before their parishes, cathedrals are desecrated by orgies, church lands are annexed by secularists, and tens of thousands of common people are executed for refusing loyalty to a vicious and arbitrary government.

And yet, the most awful part of the Revolution was not the body count. Some fates are indeed worse than death. The French Revolutionaries undertook a project so strange, so hitherto unthinkable, that many years had to pass before the effects of their work could be seen. Between 1789 and 1801, in addition to slaughtering many thousands of innocent people, the Revolutionary government attempted to systematically strip society of every reference to Christianity. Streets named for saints had their signs torn down and replaced, church buildings were seized and used for secular purposes, and the Gregorian calendar was abolished. Until 1789, French time was measured in saints' days, and each day of the year was dedicated to the memory of an event in the life of Christ, Mary, the apostles, the patriarchs, or the numberless martyrs from late antiquity and beyond. The Revolutionary government did away with the Gregorian calendar (and all the holy days which filled it) and proposed a new way of marking time. The French Republic's calendar consisted of ten-day weeks, three-week months, and a twelve-month year, with five unaccounted-for days which would be set aside as a festal season at the end of the year. The ten days of the week were all named for numbers: *primidi* (first day), *duodi* (second day), and so forth. The twelve months of the year were all renamed after natural phenomena: June 20 through July 20 were known as *Messidor* ("harvest"), July 20 through August 19 were *Fructidor* ("summer heat"), and so forth. The French Republican calendar also proposed that each day of the year be dedicated to the remembrance of flowers, fruits, farm tools, and the like: October 16 was the day of the ox, March 1 was the day of the narcissus, December 25 was the day of the dog.

This calendar was only used for around six years before France returned to the old system of marking time. Conservatives may be tempted to laugh at the failure of the French Republican calendar, for it certainly represents the delusional pride and excess which characterized the Revolution. Such laughter is naïve, however, for while the Revolutionaries failed to implement a new way of marking time, they succeeded in teaching the world a new *philosophy* of time, one which has proven to be the most demoralizing and destructive philosophy in the history of the world. Simply put, French Revolutionaries believed that man's past was behind him and that his future was in front of him.

Today, such a philosophy of time is the default position of nearly every human being in the West. When I lecture on early modern history, my students are always confused when I explain that Enlightenment philosophers and French Revolutionaries believed the past was behind them, for my students assume everyone has always believed as much. When I ask them to imagine any other possible views of man's orientation in time, they are flummoxed.

In a later chapter, I will delve further into the philosophy of time embraced by the French Revolutionaries, but before such an explanation can be meaningful, there is much to be said about the several centuries of European history which prefaced man's reorientation in time.

Origins of Secularism

The French Revolutionary view of time did not come from nowhere. It was more than a hundred years in the making. When conservative intellectuals speak contemptuously of the French Revolution, they are usually treating the Revolution as the violent culmination of Enlightenment philosophy, which began more than a century before the French beheaded Marie Antoinette and Louis XVI. While Enlightenment philosophy is expansive and complex, the sort of subject which requires much study to truly understand, one could say that overall, the Enlightenment was an attempt to unify an increasingly diverse and tumultuous world.

This diversity arose from the multitude of competing religious traditions which grew up in the century following the Reformation. Europe was populated not by Catholics and Protestants, but by Catholics, Lutherans, Calvinists, Anglicans, Anabaptists, Puritans, and Presbyterians. The latter denominations did not consider themselves all "basically Protestant" and thus all basically in agreement. Rather, in the sixteenth and seventeenth centuries, more acrimony existed between different Protestant denominations than presently exists between the Catholic Church and any single Protestant denomination. It is naïve to assume that denominational affiliations have always been as meaningless to Christians as they are today. Between the Reformation and the French Revolution, individual conversions from one tradition to another were comparatively rare, but the conversion of entire towns and regions was quite common. Violence sometimes broke out over dogmatic disagreements, but turf battles between princes of rival denominations were not uncommon either.

Throughout the Middle Ages, the average European Christian rarely entered into theological disagreements because he didn't know anyone who believed differently. A farmer in the year AD 900 might live his entire life without ever speaking to someone who was unbaptized or unchurched. All men were beholden to the same religious authority, the local bishop, and had neither the ability nor the desire to argue with the bishop about the interpretation of Scripture. The typical farmer was not educated in the modern sense of the word, which meant he had little knowledge of ancient Greece and Rome, had never read a single theory of government or statecraft (if he could read at all), and might not travel more than fifty miles from the bed on which he was conceived, born, and ultimately died. His nearest neighbors lived well out of earshot, he had little choice over whom he married, and his life was scarcely different from that of his father or grandfather. In the Middle Ages, the man born a poor French Catholic onion farmer would die a poor French Catholic onion farmer.

However, as the great cathedral-building projects of the late Middle Ages came to fruition, towns and cities grew up and men began to live closer and closer together. It takes a city to build a cathedral, but once the cathedral is finished, the city stays put. As cathedrals became more common, so did cities. In a city, education is both much cheaper and much more necessary than it is in the country. In an agrarian society wherein even the poorest farmer maintained fifteen to twenty acres of land, homes were sufficiently spread out that every student would need his own personal tutor if he wanted to learn anything his father did not already know. In a city, on the other hand, forty students might easily and quickly assemble in a classroom, thus drastically reducing the cost of knowledge. With the emergence of the city, wealth was no longer exclusively attached to land, and cash became a daily necessity. In addition to making knowledge affordable, the city also incentivized ingenuity. The medieval farmer who figured out how to build a better mousetrap might save himself the hassle of a few additional pests every year. In Renaissance Bologna, however, the man who built a better mousetrap could make a fortune, then move to Naples and make another fortune. During the Renaissance, the common man developed far greater control over his life, and after the Reformation, not only were a dazzling array of careers open to him, but a great diversity of rival denominations and creeds. By the seventeenth century, a man born a poor French Catholic onion farmer could die a rich Reformed tulip prospector in Holland.

The arrival of these new possibilities did not simply make life more interesting. Life itself was re-conceived according to new principles. In his introductory essay to *Shakespeare: The Invention of the Human*, literary critic Harold Bloom distinguishes between the manner in which persons were perceived before and after the time of Shakespeare, who reflected the growing evanescence of the West.[1] In ancient literature, characters in stories do not often undergo radical spiritual transformations. By the end of *The Song of Roland*, the titular hero is not all that different than he was in the beginning. As Roland dies, he confesses his sins, but does not regret his decision to not summon Charles for reinforcements. The same is true of Odysseus and Achilles, who are great warriors at the beginning of Homer's poems and great warriors at the end. It is tempting to think of Odysseus as an aging warrior playboy who learns to be a faithful homebody, but many readers of the Odyssey forget that the hero will leave his home a month after the narrative of the poem ends, for he has agreed to be Poseidon's missionary and spread the cult of the sea-god to people who live in the desert. Modern readers (especially Christian readers) are disappointed that Odysseus' reunion with Penelope does not also involve a confession, a reconciliation, and a renewal of vows, but the actual text of Homer's poem resists our desire to see Odysseus change. Before Shakespeare's time, characters rarely changed because human beings rarely changed, and human beings rarely changed because change—as we conceive of it today, at least—was not physically possible. The contemporary notion of simply packing up your things, skipping town, and getting a job somewhere else would make as little sense to a medieval farmer as telling a modern man marooned on an island to grow wings and fly away.

Prior to the Reformation, characters did not develop; they unfolded. Let us imagine two different ways of revealing an image. In one scenario, a man begins a sketch on a sheet of paper. At first, it appears he is drawing an ostrich, but as the sketch develops, we see it is not meant to be a real ostrich, but an image of an ostrich adorning a shield. The artist then draws a soldier holding the shield, but the artist changes his mind and decides the image of the soldier holding the shield is, in fact, just a tattoo on a man's bicep. Over the course of two hours of sketching, what began as bird undergoes a number of metaphysical changes. In the other scenario, a man has a small piece of paper which has been folded many times over, and as he unfolds it, an image begins to appear. At first, the image seems to be nothing more than geometrical shapes. But when additional pieces of the rectangle are unfolded, a city skyline appears, then the Eiffel Tower emerges, and finally what began as lines and dots is revealed to be Paris.

Broadly considered, both scenarios involve changing images; however, in the first example, the change takes place actively, presently, according to the whims of the artist. In the second example, the image was predetermined before any of it was revealed and though the viewer's knowledge of the image changed, the image itself remained unchanged. Likewise, before the modern era, characters and persons were slowly revealed like the Paris skyline, but once the modern era arrived, characters became dynamic, volatile things. Hamlet is a man whose beliefs about the world develop scene by scene. He is capable of hearing himself talk, contemplating his own words, deciding he no longer believes what he said in a previous scene, and adopting a new spiritual or intellectual posture accordingly. Neither Roland, nor Achilles, nor Odysseus did such things. The older conception of a man as a fixed, stable, fated creature had become hopelessly outdated.

The modern man cannot help seeing life beyond the Renaissance as far more free than life in the Middle Ages, but such freedom is not easy to distinguish from instability. The medieval farmer never had to defend his religious or political beliefs because he never spent time with anyone who thought differently. In much the same way, modern men never argue about the boiling point of water, the density of lead, or the distance to the moon. These matters are settled, no less settled than medieval theology, at least so far as the laity was concerned. But freedom leads to diversity and diversity leads to disagreement. After the Reformation, men and women in Europe became acquainted with a new kind of existential pain. Now, a man could go to bed every night knowing that many of his own countrymen—who spoke his language, celebrated the same holidays, and professed the same creed—nonetheless considered him a heretic bound for hell. Because conversions between traditions and denominations commonly occurred along regional divides, a man might find himself going to war over a theological quarrel which he could not personally explain. Perhaps such wars are an inevitable part of such freedom. Of Europe's two-hundred-year prelude to the French Revolution, John McManners writes:

> *Human individuality and freedom had been evolving. Religion was on its way to becoming a matter of intense personal*

decision: if there was a single message of the Reformation
and Counter-Reformation, it was this. Secularization was
the inevitable counterpart, the opposite side of the coin, the
reaction of human nature to a demand almost too intense to
bear. The idea of Christianity as some huge galleon blown
on to the rocks then pounded by the seas and plundered
by coastal predators in an age of reason and materialism
is mistaken. Christianity was itself evolving in ethos and
doctrine, finding new emphases, new inspirations . . . Euro-
pean life was being secularized; religion was becoming per-
sonalized, individualized: the two things went together, and
were interdependent.[2]

In the two centuries that followed the Reformation, each new
denomination of Christianity held on to the distinctives of their
confession with Catholic tenacity; however, as men tired of risk-
ing their lives for dogmas they hardly understood, an increasing number of Christian communities softened to pluralism
and lenience. They came to agree that divisive issues should not
be spoken of publicly. Whatever Catholics and Lutherans and
Presbyterians had in common was suited to the public square,
and their disagreements should be quarantined in the home or
the nave. Besides, there was money to be made in setting aside
religious differences. The more tolerant the shop owner, the wid-
er his customer base.

By the nineteenth century, the ethics of the public square no
longer strictly depended on any one denomination's dogma or
tradition but changed as often as the people changed, for governance of the public square had to surf on the consensus of the
various groups which composed the public. A predominantly

Catholic town could no longer be governed according to long-standing Catholic conventions but had to be stripped back and made more accommodating to an ever-expanding number of minorities. Religious dogma was no longer a sufficiently stable foundation upon which to build society. Rather, society had to be built on beliefs that cut across religious dogmas, like science and reason. As Peter Leithart suggests in *Solomon among the Postmoderns*, Catholics and Lutherans and Presbyterians could not agree on what happened to communion wine when it was consecrated, but they could all agree on the principles of fermentation.[3] Was it not obviously safer to build society on scientific principles rather than religious ones? So long as Catholic, Lutheran, and Presbyterian scientists agreed to not talk about the Eucharist, they could work together in peace.

This new peaceful, godless public square required a new sort of godless government to oversee it, and if a constantly diversifying populace was to be held together by anything other than coercion, a new godless culture was needed to bind the people together with a shared aesthetic, shared emotions, and shared virtues. As McManners notes, secularism was never foisted upon Christian people, never expelled from the public square. Rather, Christians politely agreed among themselves that religion should leave the marketplace, city hall, and theater so they could live at peace with their neighbors.[4] Secular culture was thus not an invasive species, but rather culture as Christians conceived of it after they decided that secularism was preferable to zeal.

The term "Christian art" is misleading, then, as is "religious art," for we now use both terms to denote art which is distinct from secular art. And yet, "Christian art" *was* the original secular art. Prior to the secularization of the public square, there was no "Christian art" but rather Catholic art, Presbyterian art, Anglican art, and so forth, because each saw itself as an irreducible testament to the Truth, not simply one agreeably Christian community among a host of viable alternatives. Denominations mean relatively little to most modern men (a conservative Presbyterian would sooner marry a conservative Catholic than a liberal Presbyterian), but our indifference to denominations was born out of the denominational violence of the seventeenth century. The majority of Christians today take it for granted that most theological positions are ultimately unimportant and that what matters is that Catholics, Lutherans, Presbyterians, and Baptists all "believe in Jesus." But the belief that there are non-essential truths about God—truths about God that my people believe, but other Christians are free to deny—is a concession Western Christians made several hundred years ago because they were exhausted by religious debate. Modern secular culture is constructed from the same blueprint as Christian culture of the eighteenth century. The only difference is that modern secular culture must accommodate an even greater array of religious commitments.

Enlightenment philosophers noted the economic and scientific advancements possible for a society which was willing to sequester religion to the private realm. Nonetheless, eighteenth-century monarchs doubled down on their claims to sovereignty and autonomy, even as calls for a secular form of government became more vehement. But the authority of a monarch does not so much come from God as from high-ranking clergymen, and eighteenth-century Europeans wanted the clergy to stay away from all matters of statecraft.

Besides, a religiously diverse society would never agree on

whose clergy should bestow the crown. In *The Social Contract* (1762), Jean-Jacques Rousseau consistently presented monarchy as an irrational, superstitious government suitable for children, but now European men had finally grown up, taken possession of their own souls, and were fit to decide for themselves what was best. The ancients had their chance and posterity would get their chance, so the only people whose opinions mattered were alive today, present at the table, and ready to determine the rules of the game they wanted to play. In the chilling final chapter of *The Social Contract*, Rousseau argued that Christianity was bad for the state and always had been, for Christians didn't care about earthly glory or even earthly peace. What the world needed, rather, was a new religion which was articulated so simply, so basically, no one would ever need to argue about it, debate it, or even interpret it:

The dogmas of the civil religion must be simple and few of number, expressed precisely and without explanations or commentaries. The existence of an omnipotent, intelligent, benevolent divinity that foresees and provides; the life to come; the happiness of the just; the punishment of sinners; the sanctity of the social contract and the law. These are the positive dogmas. As for the negative dogmas, I would limit them to a single one: no intolerance. Intolerance is something which belongs to the religions we have rejected . . . It is impossible to live in peace with people one believes to be damned . . .

Now that there is not, and can no longer be, an exclusive national religion, all religions which themselves tolerate others must be tolerated, provided only that their dogmas con-

tain nothing contrary to the duties of the citizen. But anyone
who dares to say "Outside the church there is no salvation"
should be expelled from the state.[5]

Traditional, conventional Christian dogmas could exist under Rousseau's civil religion provided they were entirely private, secretive, and made no difference in the public square. Of
course, Rousseau could only make such an argument because
Christians had been moving toward a secular public square for a
hundred years already: Rousseau simply put the finishing philosophical touches on an increasingly popular desire. When the
French Revolution began eleven years after Rousseau's death,
the Revolutionaries were no longer interested in melting down
every Christian denomination into a single, smooth, universally
acceptable vision of Christianity. Rather, they wanted to rid the
world of every vestige of Christianity, which meant not only at-
tacking the church but every aspect of society which the church
had a hand in creating. And so they went to war with the past.

As with all revolutionaries, the French believed that one final
cataclysmic act of violence was justifiable for the peace it would
establish. A world without Christianity and the superstitions
which invariably attended the monarchy would be governed by
sound, unshakable principles. If men were willing to leave behind the ineffective, primitive beliefs that had plunged the world
into irrational and needless violence, a new world might be created wherein peace reigned, all diseases were cured, all hunger was
ended, and men lived together without contention or poverty.

So far as Revolutionaries and Enlightenment sympathizers
were concerned, the problem was the past, which they characterized as gullible, unlearned, confused, brutal, and witless. In

the past, society was built on naïve and unprovable myths, folk tales, and fairy stories which impeded progress toward a universal peace grounded on universal principles. After many centuries of trying, Christendom had ultimately failed to offer this universality.

The Enlightenment project was doomed from the start, though, for though human beings run out of money, time, resources, energy, and desire, they never run out of the past. A war on the past will necessarily be endless, for no sooner has a man conquered the past than the very act of conquering becomes the past, as well. It is from this milieu that most mediocre art is born, which is *why it does not last.* Any society at war with the past will necessarily produce an endless tidal wave of cultural artifacts that are short-lived, for the longer any film or book or song lasts, the more adverse it is to progress. In a society bent on progress, stability is treason.

Secularism and Instability

To return to the subject of mediocrity, I should clarify again that I am not merely referring to mass-marketed, sexy IMAX spectacles of violence or to best-selling page-turners that may be fully digested in a single, hasty read. I am also referring to Enlightened morals and ethics, which are no less ephemeral than Billboard hits and box office smashes.

In 1999, *American Beauty* won Best Picture at the Academy Awards and Kevin Spacey took home Best Actor for playing Lester Burnham, a grown man who becomes sexually obsessed with Angela, the underage friend of his teenage daughter. The iconic poster of the film, which depicts a woman's bare midriff and a rose, refers to an erotic fantasy Burnham has about her. In the film, Burnham does not sleep with the girl in the end, but he does seduce her into a state of undress, kisses her, and stops just short of the act, and the film has obviously enlisted the sympathy of the audience in his project. In the original screenplay—the story which the actors agreed to shoot—Burnham and his daughter's friend do sleep together. The on-screen kiss which he and Angela share was nominated for Best Kiss at the MTV Movie Awards that year.

Many years later, Spacey's career ended after it was revealed that he had sexually exploited minors, an ironic turn of events given the role for which the actor was celebrated. Any evangelical who objected to *American Beauty* upon the film's release was condemned as a rube and a moralist who could not appreciate a good story. However, the same media outlets which initially praised the film's fashionable sexual ethics now find it also fashionable to condemn it as a vulgar display of Hollywood's old sexual recklessness. Little did they know it in 1999, but the Bible-clutching, buttoned-up prudes from flyover states were way ahead of their time.

Nonetheless, at the same time that stories of Spacey's sins came to light and the American media began their condemnations, the number-one song in the country was "bad guy" by Billie Eilish, a seventeen-year-old girl who claimed in the tune that she was the "might seduce your dad type." Unsurprisingly, the media lavished Eilish with all the praise one might expect a young female solo artist to earn for hitting the top of the charts.

So far as the zeitgeist goes, contradictions are par for the course. Fifty years ago, swimsuit competitions were in vogue; today, it is increasingly fashionable to decry swimsuit competitions as exploitative. Multiculturalism, a virtue in the 1990s, is now cultural appropriation, an embarrassing social blunder. "Color blindness," a sign of enlightenment in the Clinton years, became willful ignorance of racism in the Obama years. What American has not watched a TV show from just ten years ago and thought, "Oh, you could never say this sort of thing today"? In the 1990s, it was fashionable for professors to claim that just about every great intellectual before the twentieth century was secretly homosexual, but today, homosexuals are thought to be woefully underrepresented in the Western canon—if there even is such a thing as the Western canon. (The Academy is current-ly trying to sort out whether the Western canon even exists. If it does exist, it is bigoted, but it may be bigoted to even say it exists.) Likewise, any minority political or cultural movement which claims that "victors write the history books" has found a simple, convenient way of cynically denouncing the bias and op-pression of the majority; but when the same political movement moves beyond the tipping point and finds itself in the majority, everyone who holds out against it is told they are "on the wrong side of history." History itself comes in and out of fashion.

Art, ethics, and history are not alone in the tumult inaugurat-ed by the Enlightenment. Even science is subject to mediocrity's wild ride. In the 1990s, the USDA's Food Pyramid recommend-ed that Americans eat 6 to 11 servings of bread, cereal, rice, and pasta, but use fats and oils "sparingly." Today, everyone knows that the exact opposite is true. Pluto is a planet, then it's not, then it is. Milk is healthy, then it's not, then it is. The same goes for wine and red meat.

Such changes are not subtle refinements of prior beliefs, but complete reversals and total betrayals. The Enlightened spirit is not like a safecracker whose ear is pressed to the metal while his fingers imperceptibly turn a dial. Rather, the Enlightened spirit always needs to be tearing something down—usually whatever it created last—and the same is true of mediocre art, which is fiercely competitive and aims at unseating whatever is currently popular. Both mediocrity and the Enlightened spirit loathe permanence and fixedness. Fresh, novel prosperity must be promised with increasing rapidity. Anything which hangs around too long is liable to expose itself as a fraud or a failure.

This demand for novelty is sometimes couched in other terms, and thus progressives of our day often demand greater "diversity" in arts and letters; however, the voices which call humanities departments at colleges and classical schools to adopt a more diverse literature curriculum mean one thing by "diverse," and that is "recent." For quite some time now, Christian intellectuals have widely, happily acknowledged that Western theology is a footnote to the work of a North African man and that Western philosophy is a footnote to the work of a homosexual, or at least a man whom Academia was content to call a homosexual until just a few years ago. I refer, of course, to St. Augustine and Plato. And yet, when calls are issued for more women to be included in literature and philosophy curricula, one easily discerns that Julian of Norwich, Hildegard von Bingen, Mary Shelley, St. Clare of Assisi, Catherine of Siena, Jane Austen, George Eliot, Charlotte Brontë, Charlotte Mason, and Emily Dickinson don't count (in most people's minds) because they are old. So far as calls for diversity go, the only women who count were born in the twentieth century or later. At the same time, even these women are regularly called out by contemporary feminists for the unflattering claims they made about homosexuals, Jews, and

other minorities. Modern progressives need not make statues of
their heroes in a substance more durable than wax.

As Roger Scruton suggests in *Why Beauty Matters*, the
avant-garde of the early twentieth century was less interested in
originality than protest.[6] Many within the avant-garde thought
art of the nineteenth century was gutless, pandering, and bra-
zenly commercialistic. A robust conservative might agree with
this assessment, of course, for the more deeply Western society
committed to secularism, the fewer theological commitments
Western artists were allowed to have—and the fewer theological commitments Western artists had, the more bland and
worthless their art became. However, what began as a protest
against the banality of secularist art became a rebellion against
every tradition and artistic orthodoxy mankind ever knew. The
avant-garde began the twentieth century mocking how sentimental art had become, and they finished the twentieth century
mocking everything art had ever been.

The more vehemently the avant-garde dismissed the past,
the weirder and more snobbish it became. Thus, the twentieth
century witnessed a bifurcation in which "high art" became increasingly esoteric and "low art" became increasingly sensual.
Between World War I and the World Trade Center attacks,
high art and low art engaged in a game of chicken, wherein each
side dared the other to greater extremes. The more bizarre high
art became, the more fleshly and voluptuous was low art. Jackson Pollock and Hugh Hefner both rose to prominence in the
1950s, though Pollock's appeal was that no one understood him
and Hefner's appeal was that no one misunderstood him. When
modern men think of art, they tend to think of such highs and
lows. In the midst of this daring game of extremes, art lost the
common touch.

Endnotes

1. Harold Bloom, *Shakespeare: The Invention of the Human* (New York City: Riverhead Books, 1999)

2. John McManners, *The Oxford History of Christianity* (Oxford: Oxford University Press, 1990), 267.

3. Peter Leithart, *Solomon Among the Postmoderns* (Grand Rapids: Brazos Press, 2008), 25.

4. McManners, *The Oxford History of Christianity,* 267

5. Jean-Jacques Rousseau, *The Social Contract* (New York: Penguin Classics, 1968), 187.

6. *Why Beauty Matters*, directed by Louise Lockwood (BBC Two, 2009).

5.

Freedom

"The effect of liberty to individuals is that they may do what they please: we ought to see what it will please them to do, before we risk congratulations, which may be soon turned into complaints."
—Edmund Burke

Despite the fact that modern life has become inundated with mediocre things, the modern man still feels beholden to things of great beauty. When scanning the radio, he encounters Beethoven's Seventh Symphony on NPR, listens a moment, and thinks, "I really ought to listen to more classical music" before turning the dial to something more current and arresting. A woman picks up *Paradise Lost* in Barnes & Noble, reads a few lines from an odd page in the middle, and wistfully says to herself, "I wish I understood old books" before setting it back on the shelf and buying a lately-published novel instead. Things of great beauty inspire this sort of longing in us. When we imagine ourselves as the kind of person who loves beautiful old things, we enjoy the fantasy.

Many people feel a little bit guilty for their failure to like old books, classical music, and black and white films. We feel as though we owe it to someone—our parents, our children, our own souls—to enjoy uncommon things. If a man *wishes* he loved uncommon things, he also knows he could try to love them, and if he *tried* to love old things and succeeded, he suspects it would be worth the effort. And yet, he does not begin. "Listen to more classical music" and "Read more old books" sound like New Year's resolutions, the same kind of promises we make alongside "I will drink less," and "I will work out more." There are obviously long-term benefits to slimming down and sobering up, but much like reading *Don Quixote* or attending a Puccini opera, we know that the short-term work involves much struggle and only a little pleasure.

Of course, very beautiful things become even harder to like the more we give ourselves over to the spectacular, sexy, shocking, ultra-sensual, fashionable art and ethics of modernity. So far as acquiring good taste is concerned, balance is a myth. Every blockbuster film a man watches makes the task of reading *Paradise Lost* and *Jane Eyre* seem more dull and more pointless. Every Top Forty song he listens to makes Mozart and Bach more incomprehensible. In refusing to bear witness to the real length and breadth and depth of the human experience and insisting that life is nothing other than sex, violence, blasphemy, capital, revolution, and thrill, mediocre art not only hinders our ability to understand other people, it demands that we interpret our own lives through a laughably narrow range of emotions which are largely defined and curated by the unmarried, agnostic, pro-choice twentysomethings who now rule our culture.

Most people choose the music they listen to, the books they read, and the films they watch because of some event which has lately taken place in their own lives. People who are in love listen to love songs, people who are sad listen to sad songs, people who are angry listen to angry songs. Love songs are instructive for the young man in love because they teach him how to think about his condition and how to assign meaning to the events which occur in a romance. Sad songs teach sad people what their sadness is. Joyful songs instruct listeners on the activities and sentiments that are appropriate to joyful people. The problem is not so much that we seek art which has an affinity with our condition but we find this rapport much too easily. A mediocre song or movie asks little of us, and so it trains the heart to love, to grieve, or to be joyful in shallow, simple, and selfish ways. And in much the same way that an unpracticed and unused body will wither, bloat, and become incapable of otherwise normal tasks, so will the unpracticed and unused soul.

In a prior age, the human experience was understood as the temporal embodiment of desire, delight, fear, grief, faith, love, hope, hatred, horror, sympathy, gentleness, kindness, loyalty, fidelity, sublimity, desperation, chagrin, anger, fury, wrath, distress, discomposure, shame, dignity, indignity, glory, contempt, slight, heartbreak, fondness, tenderness, adoration, infatuation, compassion, goodwill, worship, sorrow, anguish, despair, woe, dejection, despondency, duty, angst, reverence, respect, esteem, exaltation, melancholy, disquiet, weariness, felicity, glee, bliss, ecstasy, rapture, euphoria, exhilaration, rhapsody, brotherhood, contemplation, surrender, fancy, impulse, yearning, thirst, hankering, pining, enthusiasm, need, obligation, fancy, mystery, helplessness, luck, recklessness, boldness, fearlessness, wildness, sorrow, regret, gloom, heavy-heartedness, dreaminess, and ten thousand other sensibilities. These are the sentiments which great art compels us to feel. But mediocre art truncates the human experience: it prunes and lops off the diversity and richness of life, leaving us with little more than lust, amusement, self-fulfillment, and resentment, which in turn leads to an endless search for the power that now attends victimhood. There is nothing else for modern men. Our music, our films, our books, our slogans, and our philosophies invariably funnel us toward these four banalities. The tens of thousands of other more subtle emotions can only be experienced by people who have been allowed to confront the world with their whole skin and learned the proper responses to these confrontations. But we are locked away in a dungeon of distraction and gratification. From time to time, we have the courage to admit that there is something beyond pornography and power. But in these rare moments of honesty, we confess the sad truth that we do not even want to be free. We only want to want to be free.

The great twentieth-century aphorist Nicolás Gómez Dávila once said, "Modern man is a prisoner who thinks he is free because he refrains from touching the walls of his dungeon." [1] Like many great proverbs, Dávila's claim rings true before we even know why. The idea that there is a spiritual prison which is unique to modernity cannot help but conjure up images of all the digital distractions which incarcerate the man who lives an unexamined life. We want to read and enjoy books like *Paradise Lost* and *Jane Eyre*, but the slavish habits of mind inculcated by mediocrity forbid us from attempting intellectually difficult tasks. Beyond the walls of sensual entertainment and fashionable politics, a culture of beauty and real freedom exists—but escaping the prison of mediocrity requires that we give up its undeniable comforts.

In order to understand Dávila's proverb more fully, it will be helpful to consider the life of a modern person who actually spent some time in a dungeon.

On Imprisonment

On the morning of June 10, 1991, eleven-year-old Jaycee Lee Dugard was kidnapped while walking to a school bus stop. She was taken to the residence of Phillip and Nancy Garrido, where she became their prisoner for eighteen years. Phillip Garrido claimed on many occasions to be possessed and tormented by demons, and during the first several years of her imprisonment, Dugard was often handcuffed. She was repeatedly sexually assaulted, exposed to pornography, and kept in a room which was bolted shut. She was given fast food to eat, a bucket in which to relieve herself, and a television to watch. She was not allowed to say or write her own name. Her captors offered her pets on several occasions as consolation for her loneliness, but days later they always thought better and took them away. Dugard gave birth to two daughters while imprisoned. Her daughters were eleven years old and fifteen years old when they and their mother were finally rescued from a fate that was not only worse than death, but far more confusing.

In 2011, two years after her rescue, Dugard published the memoir *A Stolen Life*,[2] wherein she describes and reflects on the eighteen years she spent in a dungeon. She also recorded an audio version of the memoir, which I listened to several years ago while driving across the country by myself. After an hour of listening, I realized that the book had almost certainly not been professionally edited. The text was unpolished, rough-hewn, and contained a host of awkward sentences. I took this to be a noble and principled move on the part of the publisher, though, for here was a woman who had not been allowed to say her own name for nearly twenty years. Who would have the gall to tell her that she was not telling her own story properly?

As the story continued, I found *A Stolen Life* to be highly unsettling for two reasons. The first, rather obviously, was that hearing a woman describe being sexually assaulted and tortured as a child was grievous and horrifying, and, as I listened, I could not help imagining such atrocities being committed against my own children. However, the book was also unsettling for another reason which I could not put my finger on until I reached the final chapters, wherein Dugard describes her rescue, her reunion with her mother, and the hobbies she took up after being freed.

Dugard's life had been "stolen," as she put it. She had not received anything beyond a fifth-grade education. She had not been allowed to attend church. She had not been given good books to read. She had not been given the chance to eat supper in the evening with people who loved her, who might ask her to reflect on her day and challenge her with intriguing questions and observations about her life and her thoughts. She had not been asked to prom. She had not been fêted on her sixteenth birthday, or her eighteenth birthday, or at graduation, or on her twenty-first birthday, and no one had thrown her a baby shower. Her understanding of the world and human nature had not been expanded and liberalized through conversations with friends, fellow adults, co-workers, neighbors, cashiers at the supermarket, and waiters at restaurants. For nearly two decades, she lost sight of human beings in their natural condition: she did not witness common people expressing love, frustration, patience, and dedication. The book of nature—by which I mean human nature and Mother Nature—was more or less closed off from Jaycee Lee Dugard, who languished in a dungeon wherein her only companions were a television and a pair of cruel captors, one of whom was a demoniac. However, what was deeply disturbing about *A Stolen Life* was that despite having missed out on all of this—despite having missed out on life itself, at least so far as "life" is normally considered—Jaycee Lee Dugard's thoughts and reflections on the world were really not all that different from what an average college student might write on an essay.

Imagine traveling to a foreign country and sitting down to interview two women, both in their late twenties. Before the two women enter the room, the man who has arranged the interview tells you that one of the two subjects was abducted as a young girl, raped, psychologically tortured, and held in captivity by maniacs until last year, when she miraculously escaped. The other woman, you are told, has lived "a normal life." Both women enter the room, and you cannot tell by looking into their eyes who has suffered more. You have been told that you may not ask either woman about her own personal history but to discuss abstractions instead. The interview begins, and you ask a series of questions about the world. You ask both women about loneliness and suffering. You ask about God and about a mother's love. You ask about hobbies and leisure, but also about injustice, freedom, bitterness. You cheat a little and make a few pointed inquiries about what they felt when they heard about the World Trade Center attacks. The interview carries on for several hours, at which point the women are dismissed from the room. The man who arranged the interview returns and asks, "Which one was kidnapped, do you think?" With great alarm, you reply, "I couldn't tell much of a difference between them."

If all this happened, what would you assume that it meant to live a "normal life" in that country?

In *A Stolen Life*, Dugard's ability to think through questions of suffering, love, hope, and justice is indistinguishable from that of people her age who have lived normally, immersed in the world of blockbuster films, disposable fashion, popular music, easy virtue, virtue signaling, screen addiction, trendy political causes, and banal propaganda. The further I got into *A Stolen Life*, the more I realized that Dugard sounded just like the young women (and men) whose work I read in college writing workshops. My conclusion is both horrifying and offensive: for all the good our freedom is doing us, we might as well be locked up in a dungeon with a demoniac. The effects of living freely in the modern world are not easily distinguishable from the effects of living in captivity with a psychopath.

Preferring Incarceration

A man is only as free as his love of good things. The modern world is arranged such that a free man with a moderate salary can more or less purchase the life of an inmate for himself, and he may even prefer this to a conventional life of freedom. The life of an inmate is chiefly characterized by confinement to a small space, and modern life is ever more characterized by a reticence to leave home. The inmate might take his meals in his cell, and the modern man is rapidly coming to prefer that his food be delivered as opposed to sitting in a restaurant and eating a meal in the company of others. An inmate spends most of his days under surveillance (or mulling over the possibility he is under surveillance), and the same is true of the free man who spends his days online. It is well known that sexual abuse and degradation are common in American prisons, and it is just as well known that the internet is a prolific and profoundly effective pornography distribution system. If violence is common in American prisons, it must also be noted that violent virtual fantasies are a common hobby of many young men and women, though we excuse them because they transpire in digital space and thus there is no bloody mess to clean up later. With each passing decade, mediocrity makes the difference between freedom and incarceration a little less distinct.

Modern men rarely attempt the sort of leisure activities that were emblematic of freedom before the French Revolution—the concept of "leisure" as it was commonly understood just a hundred years ago is no less obsolete today than concepts like spontaneous generation and phrenology. The typical modern man rarely reads old books or listens to old music, and he walks through a gallery in an art museum as quickly as he scrolls through images on Instagram. He might feel free, but a man cannot truly claim that he is "free to enjoy beauty" if he has so corrupted and starved his soul that it can no longer receive pleasure from it. Disregard for the soul's existence affects his ability to enjoy truly good things, for they appeal to both mind and soul. Even many Christians are disinterested in tending the soul. We enjoy the idea that our souls will go to be with God when we die, but we are not terribly concerned that they should accomplish anything before then. Neither do we care what condition our souls are in when they go to be with God, for we believe that the effect of dying has an instantaneous, painless, purgatorial effect on our souls. The average Christian is so unconcerned with his soul during life, it is a wonder we take any consolation at the thought that our souls go to God after death—it's a little like hearing that our neckties will go to be with God when we die.

However, merely saying that modern men "rarely attempt to read old books" is only half the story. The fact remains that something in the heart of a modern man (a still, small voice) desperately wishes to understand and enjoy old things, and yet something else in his heart revolts against them because of the hierarchical politics and religiosity which he knows were necessary to create them. Most Americans know that the hierarchical politics of old—by which I mean kings and queens and dukes and duchesses—did not hold that all men are created equal but that some men are born more important than others. What is more, hierarchical politics are inconsistent with the belief that all opinions are equally valid, or that art is fundamentally about self-expression, or that beauty is subjective, or that judging another person's taste is rude, or any of the other egalitarian views of art which keep modern men from taking moral responsibility for the art they create and patronize. Neither did the hierarchical religiosity of old encourage every individual to read the Scriptures daily and determine for himself what Genesis or St. John's Gospel means. The hierarchical religiosity of old did not endlessly lament "the state of the church today," as though the individual were competent to critique the church and solve problems which "organized religion" had bungled time and time again. Rather, the politics and religion capable of producing Mozart's Requiem or St. Peter's Basilica or the Hagia Sophia are almost entirely gone (as is the belief that Mozart's Requiem constitutes a fitting funeral for one lately departed from this life). St. Peter's Basilica is the fruit of numerous theological dogmas that are now thought obsolete, uncouth, and pretentious.

But modern beliefs about politics, church government, democracy, and so forth are all neatly and appropriately reflected in modern literature, music, and liturgies. We do not deserve a better culture than the one we have; every culture is perfectly suited to the music it produces, the churches it builds, and the poems it writes. We cannot lament our inability to build a fitting sequel to St. Peter's Basilica without simultaneously lamenting our complete lack of a theology that might compel us to do so.

A man is free to do good to the extent that he does good. If a man claims he could do good, but doesn't do it, he either doesn't know what goodness is or he doesn't know what freedom means. Many men wish they were free, but upon experiencing the responsibilities and ideological commitments that come with freedom, they shrink back in fear. The dungeon of which Nicolás Gómez Dávila wrote is not a physical dungeon, but a spiritual one, and it is a dungeon created by the banalities, trivialities, and absurdities of modern life, all of which breed in men a spirit of timidity, fear, dullness, boredom, and sloth. Unlike physical dungeons, spiritual dungeons cannot be forced upon a man. He must willingly accept a spiritual dungeon, and from the point he accepts it, he may become habituated to it, prefer it, and finally hate anything other than imprisonment.

Prior to the twentieth century, a man's life might have been made miserable through war, famine, invasion, pestilence, disease, disobedient children, a cruel king, or a heartless spouse—and yet none of these miseries necessarily robbed a man's life of purpose, for the Cross is not an aberration, but the foundation of reality. Following the Enlightenment, however, the misery of American and European men came less from violence and starvation than from the vapid, soul-corrupting triteness of his culture.

Thus, before any conversation about art can be valuable, it must be admitted that what is now called "art" and what was called "art" in a bygone era—before the French Revolution, let us say—are not exactly the same. If read the first canto of *The Divine Comedy* and then read the first chapter of *The Maze Runner*, you will intuit that while both are stories, the difference between them is not just one of degree. *The Divine Comedy* is not just better than *The Maze Runner*. If we are willing to say that *The Maze Runner* ought to be read, it is hard to say that *The Divine Comedy* ought to be read as well. Whatever Dante wants of us, it is radically different.

Truth, Goodness, Beauty, and Choice

Having taught art history for many years, I can say that when the majority of students think about art, they think first of artists like Pollock, Kandinsky, and de Kooning, whose esoteric works regularly make national news for achieving astronomical price tags. Ostensibly, these incomprehensible price tags suggest incomprehensible genius, which makes many common people think art a thing which is over their heads, and so they despair of ever understanding it. After all, the people who pay a hundred million dollars for a canvas of paint splatters must have earned all that money through some authentic genius of their own. Anyone cunning enough to make a fortune would not be foolish enough to throw it all away, would they?

My students commonly waver between two incompatible theories of art. On the one hand, they think of art as a thing which needs to be understood, and because paintings by Pollock, Kandinsky, et al., make no sense to them, they believe they are incapable of enjoying sophisticated art. They have, perhaps, read a stray paragraph here or there which "explains" Pollock's *Greyed Rainbow* or *Autumn Rhythm*, but because the explanation was full of rarefied descriptions and obscure terminology, they feel embarrassed to express any opinion at all about Botticelli's *Birth of Venus* or the *Mona Lisa*.

On the other hand, students also commonly claim that "beauty is in the eye of the beholder" because they feel as strongly about Post Malone or Ed Sheeran as some adults feel about Bach's *Goldberg Variations*. Plus, the idea that beauty is purely subjective seems generous. It affords every man's opinion inalienable dignity and has the convenient side-effect of meaning that their own taste cannot be judged.

As opposed to viewing art as a human enterprise which can (and must) unite the heart and the mind, students buy simultaneously into two incompatible theories: that art is full of cryptic symbols which are suited only to specialists, and that art is universally adaptable to every human desire, no matter how stupid or wicked. The problem, of course, is that neither of these views is capable of penetrating to the soul, which means that the work of populists and obscurists alike leads to alienation and disenchantment.

In order to gain (or recover) a proper understanding of art, we must look back further than the twentieth century, even further than the war against high culture which formally broke out in the French Revolution, and instead examine a world which was established to adore Truth, Goodness, and Beauty. Since World War I, modern men have lived under the "cult of ugliness," as Sir Roger Scruton once put it, and so we should expect this older world wherein men served the cult of beauty to offend our most deeply-held beliefs about freedom, originality, autonomy, and power.[3] We should not expect beauty to cater to us. We should prepare to bow down.

Prior to the nineteenth century, the ability to create great works of art was not likely to make anyone rich. Artists competed for the sponsorship of wealthy patrons rather than the general public, so in order for an artist to survive, he had to impress someone who was educated in history, literature, philosophy, theology, and statecraft. A system of aristocratic patronage was necessary in a time before mass culture and mass marketing, and prior to the twentieth century, art could not be easily commodified and exported. The only way to hear a man play a piano was to be in the same room with him. Similarly, seeing a famous painting required a pilgrimage to the painting's physical location, and the same was true of bazaars, fairs, circuses, and plays. Thus, audiences were small and artists depended upon the generosity of the upper class. (Although "local authors" and "local bands" exist to this day, if their appeal is dependent upon their localness, this limits their audience to such a point that few survive on book or record sales alone.)

Given such an arrangement, patrons did not need the art which they sponsored to appeal to the public—their personal fortunes were unaffected by public opinion of their collections. Rather, the art which was sponsored by the aristocracy taught the public what was good, and the public—butchers and bakers and candlestick makers, all of whom were trained exclusively within their fields of labor—accepted the fact that their lack of education in history, theology, literature, and so forth made them relatively poor judges of beauty. They were humble enough to rely on the good taste of others.

The wealthy patrons who funded musicians, painters, poets, and architects would not recoup their expenses from the public, for when such art was shared, it was done so without charge, for the benefit of those who came to view or hear it. When a father plays his children Bach and Debussy or when a teacher shows his students the paintings of Botticelli, neither the father nor the teacher expect to get rich because the recipients like what they are offered. They do so purely for the benefit of their audience. An experienced teacher does not pass out copies of *Paradise Lost* and tell the class, "You're going to love this book," because the feelings of a lot of teenagers about a classic work of literature really don't matter. Reading *Paradise Lost* is no more fun than going to church: a few students will someday love *Paradise Lost*, but only after much struggle and unpleasant discipline.

Rather, the teacher gives his students *Paradise Lost* because the book is good, and because goodness is rare, and unless someone with experience and authority commends good things to the young and naïve, they will remain ignorant of goodness. The teacher handing out *Paradise Lost* should tell his students, "This is one of the greatest books ever written. It is wise and beautiful," and then the students will understand that they *ought* to like the book. If they do not like the book, the problem is not with the book, but with their own hearts. Simply put, they do not yet know how to feel about the world, but a good education begins to remedy this, just as it remedies ignorance.

In the absence of such an education, choice becomes overwhelming, and the rising number of choices without any governance as to which is superior to another leaves a man more indecisive, more slothful, and harder to please. In the 1950s, a man had the choice to watch a TV show or not, but the TV station decided what that show would be with some concern for both quality and popularity. Today, a man has very few limitations as to which TV shows he can watch, but more choices have not made him happier—even if some of the options are good. Ideally, there would be very few shows on TV and they would *all* be good, but in order for this to happen, the possibility of TV stations becoming fabulously rich would have to be removed from the equation, for they would need to be unconcerned with popularity. Also, a well-trained, well-qualified governing body would have to make difficult decisions about what did and didn't deserve to be shown. This, however, presupposes an aristocracy, or at least the same sort of aristocratic arrangement we find in a family, wherein some people's opinions inherently matter more than others.

Like a father or a teacher, such a governing body would not shape culture around pleasure alone. A good teacher disciplines the hearts and minds of his students and "no discipline is pleasant at the time," (Heb 12:11) as St. Paul teaches. While self-discipline is not impossible, it is not common, and if we admit that wisdom is rare, we must also admit that wisdom will rarely be the outcome of a popular vote. And yet, ours is a culture wherein music and books and motion pictures are created on the basis of a popular vote. This does not mean that beauty is altogether absent in the modern world, but it does mean that in a democracy, an unexamined life will usually be quite ugly. In the sort of agrarian life typical during the Middle Ages, "going with the flow" meant following the invariable rhythms of nature and the human traditions which tamed nature. In the modern age, though, "going with the flow" means consuming only the most

popular amusements and expressing only the most popular beliefs about morality and politics.

Aristocratic Arrangements

At this point, I have openly made a host of appreciative comments about an aristocratic arrangement of society, and before
going further, I would like to make a few caveats and qualifi-
cations. First, my interest in an aristocratic social arrangement
has very little to do with politics. I do not wish to see America attempt to reform along more ancient principles of government. Instead, I believe that living up to the sufficiently noble
principles upon which this country was founded is as much a
challenge as we can presently handle. We should not attempt
anything more difficult, nor is violent revolution the answer. I
am not fond of movements and oppose all those who attempt to
"change the world," especially when they believe they are changing it for the better.

Second, following the central metaphor of Plato's *Republic*,
I believe that every distinct form of government (monarchy,
democracy, and so forth) is the incarnation of very particular
dogmas which describe human nature. While the *Republic* ostensibly deals with theories of government, Plato was less interested in how all men should be governed than he was in how an
individual man ought to govern his soul. Monarchy, aristocracy,
democracy, fascism, socialism, and republicanism are, first and
foremost, beliefs about what a man is and under what sort of
circumstances he thrives. In this, a man might live under a socialist form of government and yet govern his own soul like an
aristocrat, or a monarch, or a republican, or what have you.

When I refer to "governing one's own soul," I mean the manner in which a man assigns meaning and importance to all the people, places, and things in the world. Does he primarily value stability or progress? The prevention of crime or the punishment of criminals? Is he more inclined to trust the rich or the poor? The educated city-dweller or the simple rustic? Does a man want to be admired by his neighbors or does he simply want to be left alone? What does he want from his leisure hours—sensuality or intellection? Industry or indolence? And does a man usually put his trust in what is oldest or what is newest? What is ubiquitous or what is obscure? What is obvious or what is subtle? Or, how does a man govern his desires: as a general governs his soldiers, as a father governs his children, as a restaurateur governs his employees, as a radio station DJ governs his playlist, or as the creative director at H&M governs the cut of jeans being released this fall?

For years, I have argued to my students that loving good things requires that we govern our souls like aristocrats, although I begin this argument by asking, "What did aristocrats do?" and I speak in the past tense, for the aristocrat is more or less extinct. The general consensus among students is that aristocrats attended balls, drank tea, and did little else. They inherited massive fortunes and never did any work, and thus they were all arrogant and self-obsessed. These opinions are helped by many period films which depict aristocrats as immoral and ignorant, whereas their butlers are clever, upright Christian fellows who deserve to have the power and money instead. Above all, the average modern American understanding of the aristocracy suggests that a profound chasm separated the upper crust of society from the lowly laborers, a chasm which the aristocracy was only too happy to deepen every chance they got. And so they maliciously sipped their cognac from crystal chalices whilst their serfs and tenants—each one a Tiny Tim or Oliver Twist— died of exhaustion, malnutrition, consumption, and starvation.

However, the aristocratic arrangement of society prior to the French Revolution did not mean a hard and fast line was drawn between aristocrats and common people, for both the aristocracy and the peasantry depended on one another. The peasantry made life possible and the aristocracy made life *good*.

If life is reduced to just a beating heart, we would have to agree that the aristocracy served no purpose for they did not produce anything, which is to say they were not useful. Beauty is not useful, for it lies beyond usefulness. Beauty gives meaning and inspires loyalty: we need useful things, but we love beautiful things. A building which is merely functional will not last, for people will not love it. They will get bored with it. Every NFL stadium which has opened in the last decade has cost more a billion dollars to build[4] although they're not likely to last more than nineteen,[5] after which they appears dated and unfashionable. The Chartres Cathedral, on the other hand, is more beautiful than any sports complex on earth and it has been functional for more than eight hundred years. Beautiful things last because when they begin to fall apart, we tend to them, revive them, and restore them; however, when purely functional things fall apart, we tire of them and replace them.

In *Why Beauty Matters*, Sir Roger Scruton notes that every major metropolis the world over has an impoverished district wherein the buildings are covered in graffiti. These buildings are ugly, but as purely functional, soulless boxes, they were ugly long before they were graffitied. Because no thought was taken for the aesthetics of such buildings, the graffiti which finally covers them is not really vandalism, but a dare. The so-called vandal says, "I dare you to find a reason to remove this graffiti." If a building is designed merely to keep the wind and the rain out with no concern for delighting the soul, there is no reason to remove the graffiti, for it does not detract from the building's functionality. Winston Churchill once said, "We shape our buildings; thereafter they shape us." If the architect does not confirm that the inhabitants of his building have souls, they will usually come to agree and ultimately prove their agreement through their behavior. But if the architect treats the inhabitants as dignified ladies and gentlemen, they are also likely to agree and to act likewise. The aristocracy understood this and—in return for the money that they took from the public—they made life better for those who gave it through music, through architecture, and through art.

In an aristocratic era, a common man could go to the theater or gallery knowing that what he heard and saw was good enough for the best men. Beethoven and Bach and Botticelli made kings and common men companions, of a sort. Men of labor and men of leisure met in the middle, which is the space where art and culture dwell. Christians understood that kings and peasants were united by metaphysical, ontological bonds and that these bonds both humbled kings and exalted the lowly. The existence of any aristocrat proves that all men have aristocratic blood. The king is not wholly other than the people—the king is an icon of every person's regal nature.

When the French Revolutionaries executed Louis XVI and Marie Antoinette, deposed the aristocracy, and stripped the Catholic Church of its privileges and lands, they imagined that the end of the ancien régime would elevate common people to places of high dignity that kings and queens, dukes and duchesses, priests and bishops had been selfishly hoarding for hundreds of years. But glory and dignity are not commodities and cannot be redistributed any more than knowledge can be collected from human brains and redistributed. *Books* can be redistributed, but knowledge requires a desire to read. So, too, money can be redistributed, but only those who want to spend it prudently will benefit from it, and the desire to spend money prudently will always be more rare than money itself.

In putting an end to kings and queens, the French Revolutionaries also put an end to kingly and queenly behavior. If kings and queens are oppressive and unjust and deserve banishment, then common men should no longer treat their wives like queens and common women should no longer treat their husbands like kings. After vanquishing the highest realms of dignity and honor, the public became disoriented. There was nothing real before them which they could imitate. Doing away with dukes and duchesses did not elevate the peasantry: the peasantry had destroyed all the places to which they might have been elevated. Dignity had not been redistributed, it had simply been destroyed. The French were left with nothing but theories, and no one loves a theory—a person is rightly offended when he intuits someone is treating him according to a theory, for theories apply to objects, not free persons. And so, having thrown down and debased everyone who was worthy of imitation, the Revolutionaries would ultimately go on to preach, "Be yourself," a dismal and reluctant slogan which is only appropriate to a society wherein no one is worthy of imitation.

Of course, the self is subject to endless incarnations, none of which lasts terribly long. Before a man can be himself, he must find himself, and finding oneself often means adopting a fashionable persona: jock, preppy, queer, revolutionary, stoner, hipster. Each is accompanied by a readily identifiable style of dress, a few lately published books, a little insider lingo, and half a dozen musical purchases. For around $300 and a few hours on Wikipedia, anyone can acquire an entirely new self. And yet, we also tire of being ourselves, which makes us want to lose ourselves and begin again. People who want to find themselves, people who want to lose themselves, and people who want to be themselves tend to end up in the same places, doing the same things, for all three activities usually involve sex, drugs, and violence. The self—the existential center of Revolutionary ideology—thus seems little more than a nullifying force of needless confusion and misdirection, for no one knows whether it is coming, going, or staying put.

Aristocratic Metaphysics

In his remarkable essay "Sin No More," Remi Brague argues that the division between aristocrat and common man is established in the creation week.[6] On the Sabbath, man refrains from the work which makes life possible and is free to pursue the good of the soul, which, for modern-day Christians, is principally accomplished through liturgical, ecclesiastical worship. Brague writes that "the Sabbath is free time, time for leisure . . . for the activities that become a free man. The ancient thinkers . . . drew a line between what becomes a free man and what we are compelled to do in order to keep things going: tilling the soil, building houses, weaving garments, cooking meals, etc." All those labors which a man performed in order to keep his body alive were "servile," whereas those labors which kept the soul alive were "liberal arts." In this way, even King Adam and Queen Eve were nonetheless involved in servile work, for they had to tend their garden and harvest fruit in order to stay alive.

And yet, while productive work is important to God, He has far higher priorities. As John Milton points out in book IX of *Paradise Lost*, if God were anxious to see the earth filled and subdued, He would have created more than two people and He would not have appointed a day of rest. God has interests for man which transcend "getting things done." Thus, the Sabbath is not merely free time, but time to be an aristocrat—time to set aside all those labors which make life possible and to pursue, instead, those things which make life good. The Sabbath was not viewed as a reward for hard work or a bonus for worshiping Yahweh (the Ten Commandments forbid the Israelites from requiring anyone to do work on the Lord's Day, even pagans, for pagans also have souls which need tending). The Sabbath confirmed the aristocratic nature of all human beings.

Sadly, much of what is now considered "leisure" would have been regarded as sloth in bygone eras. Because modern men are skeptical that the soul exists, they tend to think of "free time" as time to do whatever they want, which might be anything from fishing to dancing to watching six hours of television. Americans now associate "leisure" with eating a bucket of popcorn and drinking an aquarium of Coca-Cola while reclining in an air-conditioned theater and watching women in latex catsuits recklessly battle aliens, robots, and mutants until New York City is destroyed. A hundred years ago, when Americans thought of leisure, they thought of learning to play the viola or reading poetry. Until quite recently, in fact, "leisure" referred to those things which could expand and enrich the soul. In the *City of God*, St. Augustine equates leisure with the "consideration of truth or the quest for it"[7] and not "lazy inactivity."[8] Thus, a proper use of leisure time might involve the enjoyment or composition of music, the creation of art or sculpture, the authoring and reading of literature, or participation in certain sports. None of these activities sustain a man's body, at least not in the way that thatching a roof, planting a garden, milking a cow, or darning a sock sustain the body. The composition of a poem confers no material advantage to the author, and it would be ridiculous to imagine a scenario in which a woman responded to a lover's poem with cash. Rather, the activities appropriate to leisure are those which set aside material practicalities for the sake of the soul.

On Spiritual Slavery

As Brague notes elsewhere in "Sin No More," the law is given to the Israelites only after they have been delivered from Egypt, where they served the material needs of their tyrannical masters. The Ten Commandments are thus a kind of Gentleman's Code, the standard for "taking one's freedom seriously." This same exodus from Egypt is sacramentally lived out in every Christian baptism, for in accepting baptism, every Christian enlists his soul in a mythology of slavery and liberation. That mythology goes something like this:

In ancient times, all men were kings and queens, and we knew that our real father was a king from another world who walked with us in the cool of the evening. Then one day, one of our own kind betrayed us and sold us as slaves to the Devil, our father's mortal en-

emy. *The Devil put us in chains and led us from our Garden home to his plantation of Death. And every morning, for thousands of years, the Devil dressed as an admiral and stood on the porch of his manor house, with his arms folded, as we were sent into the fields to lust and envy and furtively stuff our mouths with ash when no one was looking. A wall made of concrete and iron engulfed the plantation and we dreamed of the freedom on the other side. Over the centuries, we forgot who we really were. We went from a race of kings to a race of amnesiacs. Every day, our toil was pointless, and all the grain we harvested was poisonous and rotten.*

But after many thousands of years, our real father (the king from that other world) returned and knocked down the high walls which kept us trapped in the Devil's plantation. To this day, he beckons us to leap over the rubble and reclaim our ancient right to rule the world as kings. Everyone who crosses over the rubble must first take a coronation oath and confess a litany of ancient vows (many mysterious things, many sacred stories), then the newly liberated are given white robes befitting the angels. For all those who make it to the other side of the razed wall, there is a place of brightness, a world of verdure, a haven of repose ready for us. Yet, there are plenty who, having worn the crown and the white robes, look back and want to return to the plantation to get one last taste of the ash, one last chew of fat from a bloated corpse which has lain in the sun for weeks.[9]

Ancient Christians did not see baptism as a needlessly formal declaration of loyalty, but rather as a kind of spiritual operation. Imagine, for a moment, that over a period of many months a certain man becomes increasingly sick and finally makes an appointment with a doctor. After running many tests and collecting many samples, the doctor tells the man, "Your kidney is being devoured by cancer. Something inside of you is dying, and if we do not remove the dying thing, the rest of you will die with it. So we are going to open you up, take out the dead thing, and give you a living organ instead." The doctor does this. He removes the dying kidney and sows part of the body of another human being inside the dying man's body. When the man wakes from surgery, he is not the same person. Now, he is two. He will die with a body that derived from two different mothers.

Baptism is no less radical, no less bizarre. However, baptism is not the cure for a failing kidney or heart or liver, but a failing nature. Captivity to the Devil sets mankind on a path toward eternal death, and the man who dies without a divine nature has no means by which to conquer death once he has gone to the realm of the dead. Baptism is the operation wherein a man's human nature is drowned out of him and the nature of God replaces his old one. When a man emerges from the waters of baptism, he is not the same kind of creature he was before. He is not merely human, because that which is sowed inside him is God himself.

"Be careful," says the doctor to the man who has just received a new kidney. "Be careful," says the priest to the newly baptized. "You are now free to act in accord with the new nature which has been given you. It will allow you to do things you could not do before—things you have always wanted to do but did not have the strength to do. Likewise, there are things you could do before the operation which you cannot do now without terrible repercussions. I warn you, if you act against the new nature which has been sown into you, your life may be even worse than it was before."

The freedom from the world which God grants in baptism is not the right to live like slaves beyond the gates of the Devil's plantation. This freedom is a way of life, a style of life, attended by a whole battery of tastes, words, renunciations, suffering, service, and contemplation. And yet, the soulless entertainments of the Devil's plantation—of the dungeon—are still available.

Endnotes

1. At the moment, none of Dávila's longer works are readily available in English, and I have only been able to encounter his thought through online collections of quotes and proverbs translated by enthusiasts. If interested, the Goodreads page devoted to Dávila is a good place to start.

2. Jaycee Dugard, *A Stolen Life: A Memoir* (New York: Simon & Schuster, 2011).

3. *Why Beauty Matters*, directed by Louise Lockwood (BBC Two, 2009). https://vimeo.com/549715999.

4. "NFL Stadium Comparisons," *Stadiums of Pro Football*, https://www.stadiumsofprofootball.com/comparisons/(accessed February 8, 2023).,

5. Don Muret, "The Shrinking NFL Stadium Lifespan," *Venues Now*, June 13, 2022, https://venuesnow.com/the-shrinking-nfl-stadium-lifespan/.,

6. Remi Brague, "Sin No More," *The American Spectator*, May 1, 2008, https://spectator.org/42037_sin-no-more/.

7. St. Augustine, *City of God*, trans. Henry Bettenson (London: Penguin Classics, 1972) 847

8. *Ibid.*, 880.

9. I am indebted to David Bentley Hart for inspiring this comparison in "The Great Rebellion," chapter 10 of *Atheist Delusions: The Christian Revolution and Its Fashionable Enemies* (New Haven: Yale University Press, 2009).

6.

On Beauty

"Hierarchies are celestial. In hell all are equal."
                                        —Nicolás Gómez Dávila

Most discussions of beauty begin with philosophy and metaphysics and lean heavily toward the academic and theological end of things. They open with the music of Bach and the paintings of Botticelli before moving into easily recognizable attributes of beautiful things, such as harmony, symmetry, proportion, and so forth. The differences between artistic and moral beauty are clarified, and then the conversation invariably turns toward the innate human yearning for beauty. I have benefited greatly from books that carry on as such, but I would like to begin my own discussion of the beauty of uncommon things with the most offensive and dangerous beauty there is: the physical beauty of human beings. No honest conversation about the beauty of Bach's and Botticelli's works can be had until we confess a host of uncomfortable truths about human beauty.

In *The Beauty of the Infinite*, David Bentley Hart writes:

*There is . . . an undeniable ethical offense in beauty: not only
in its history as a preoccupation of privilege, the special concern of an economically and socially enfranchised elite, but
in the very gratuity with which it offers itself. There is an unsettling prodigality about the beautiful, something wanton
about the way it lavishes itself upon even the most atrocious
of settings, its anodyne sweetness often seeming to make the
most intolerable of circumstances bearable: a village ravaged
by pestilence may lie in the shadow of a magnificent mountain's ridge: the marmorean repose of a child lately dead of
meningitis might present a strikingly piquant tableau; Cam-
bodian killing fields were often lushly flowered. . . . Beauty
seems to promise a reconciliation beyond the contradictions
of the moment, one that perhaps places time's tragedies within a broader perspective of harmony and meaning.[1]*

Hart's "unsettling prodigality" is nowhere more unsettling
than in the human form, for there is no discernible connection
between physical beauty and spiritual goodness, as is evidenced
by the fact that many of the world's most beautiful human beings cluster around Hollywood and yet Hollywood is also an
icon of all that is vacuous and empty in American culture. Many
of the world's most beautiful people do not seem particularly
righteous or happy, for scandal, divorce, addiction, and fear come
readily with fame, and fame constantly hangs about those who
are physically beautiful.

Christians find the costly and inefficient nature of beauty offensive, and so they often avoid psychologically realistic conversations about physical beauty by talking instead about "spiritual
beauty," which is better understood as goodness or holiness. An

egalitarian culture (which is no longer particular to progressives but *de rigueur* among conservative Christians, as well) cannot fail to hate beauty, for beauty is riotously unfair. As America becomes more acclimatized to socialist thought, the less talent will be allowed to matter. The late aggrandizement of pretentious hacks like Jackson Pollock and Mark Rothko betrays the progressive's frustration with the inequalities which beauty invariably establishes. The average man sees an ugly avant-garde painting, learns it sold for a hundred million dollars, and cannot help responding, "But I could have painted that," which is exactly the point. In the end, the progressive and the modern Christian argue the same thing: beauty is not physical or sensual. The modern Christian wants beauty to be spiritual and the modern progressive wants it to be intellectual, both of which make beauty democratic and easily accessible. If a man is just smart enough or just good enough, he can be beautiful, too.

Both positions are gnostic, though, and avoid an honest confrontation with the world.

While we are quick to draw a heavy line between artistic beauty and physical beauty, little divides the two: both are unnecessary, both are mesmerizing, both are offensive. Nevertheless, physical beauty is eminently more impressive, visceral, and humbling than artistic beauty. Were a human being the likes of Nicole Kidman or Paul Newman to stand on display in the Metropolitan or the Louvre, and were patrons of the museum able to gaze with impunity—not covertly and from a distance, but from point-blank range as though the living spectacles were mere portraits—many people would quickly leave behind the artistic beauty of Rembrandt and Titian.

And yet, we cannot gaze with impunity, because there are

rules of shame and propriety which govern the enjoyment of human beauty. These rules are not anomalous but are discernible within the realm of artistic beauty, as well. All beauty places a burden on those who bear witness to it. The burden is an obligation to declare that it has been seen. If two people stand before a Rembrandt painting long enough, one will have to say, "This is beautiful," to the other. Likewise, if a husband and wife dine in a restaurant wherein their waitress is very beautiful, both man and woman feel awkward until one acknowledges the fact. Neither feels as though they can be honest with the other and get on with the business of the meal until one person admits, "The waitress is very beautiful." Making this declaration alleviates the obligation: a man is relieved to admit that great beauty has come near, since confessing its presence recalibrates reality after it has been thrown askew. Silence in the presence of beauty is simply intimidation.

Beauty is naturally confrontational, for we must encounter beauty before we can believe it is real. While the maxim "Beauty is in the eye of the beholder" strikes some traditionalists as pure relativism, in various treatises on the subject, Roger Scruton argues that between truth, beauty, and goodness, beauty is something of an odd man out.[2] The irregular place of beauty among the three transcendentals owes to the fact that beauty must be experienced directly, while we are willing to acknowledge truth and goodness by way of a proxy. We may come to believe that a certain man is good by the testimony of witnesses, even though we have not met the good man personally. For example, I am willing to recommend a certain auto mechanic to my friends because I have heard credible testimony about the mechanic from others, even if he has never serviced my car. "You should take your car to that good mechanic over in Lakeside," I say, even though I don't know him from Adam. Likewise, truth may be also established by witnesses (as in a court of law), but also by the nature of logic. Because of logic, I believe that you, my reader, are mortal even though we have never met face to face.

On the other hand, people are generally unwilling to grant that a thing is beautiful unless they have laid their own eyes on it. If Tom tells Harry, "I was cold today and a stranger gave me the coat off his back," Harry might reply, "What a good man!" However, if Tom tells Harry, "I saw a beautiful woman today at the flower shop," Harry cannot reply, "What a beautiful woman!" If someone claims that a certain symphony of Beethoven's is beautiful, we assume he has heard the symphony—if he has not, we take him for a liar. He may report that his friends have heard the symphony and claim it is beautiful, but this is not enough because the assessment that a thing is beautiful implies (and demands) a personal confrontation.

In this way, "Beauty is in the eye of the beholder" does not mean every man is free to determine beauty on his own terms. Rather, beauty is the point at which knowledge of God must be tasted, not merely acknowledged by way of rational assent. Proportion, harmony, and symmetry might be found floating around in the ethereal realm of platonic forms, but the knowledge of beauty comes only by way of incarnation.

Because beauty must be confronted, it possesses the power to pacify, sublimate, and terrify. Beauty is a liability. "Beauty will save the world," but don't tell the Trojans that or they may reply, "Save the world? Beauty is tearing the world apart!" Any starry-eyed messiah quoting Dostoevsky from the walls of Troy would have been pitched over. The beauty of Helen threw the cosmos out of whack. The beauty of Sarai jeopardized Abram's trip into Egypt. A beautiful sunbather may upset the peace of a family trip to the beach, and a beautiful priest might easily distract from mass or compromise confession.

Utopianism and Beauty

Because beauty is gratuitous and does not serve a practical or necessary function, the creation of beautiful things always means some useful task must remain undone. For this reason, artistic beauty is no less offensive, jarring, unfair, and embarrassing than human beauty. In Mark 16, when Mary anoints Christ's feet with perfume, Judas asks why the perfume wasn't sold and the money given to the poor. Judas' motives were compromised, for his concern was not the poor but himself, but we may readily imagine the question being asked honestly. Why, indeed? Christ's reply that the woman has done "a beautiful thing" and that "the poor you will always have with you" indicates that the Christian duty to be generous is not meant as a solution to the problem of human suffering. Although charity money should be distributed in a competent manner to maximize the good of the donation, the giving of alms has more to do with healing the spirit of the giver than healing the body of the one who receives. Alms which fail to eliminate poverty are not wasted.

Nonetheless, there are those who argue that no church building should be beautiful until all the parishioners are fed and clothed. "Whoever has two tunics is to share with him who has none," teaches St. John the Baptist (Luke 3:11), and yet the local priest has seven sets of costly vestments while the homeless are dressed in rags. Those who argue that the creation of beautiful

things means robbing the poor of their due—and that the poor
are the rightful owners of all the wealth that the church hoards
in gold chalices, Gothic cathedrals, and magnificent artwork—
assume that beauty really does no one any good at all.

But where does the impulse to give to the poor come from? Is it
self-derived? Or is it born of bearing witness to a society wherein
the gratuity and generous overflow of beauty is witnessed in art
and architecture, public parks, libraries full of beautiful books
and music, and glorious cathedrals? In other words, the value of
every beautiful thing *could* be liquidated and the money given to
the poor, but after every church and cathedral has been stripped
of its beauty, will those who worship therein still feel the same
impulse to give? If every public park and library were convert-
ed into public housing, every park bench used to fuel fires that
warmed the poor, and every museum's endowment requisitioned
for soup kitchens, would anyone want to live in the gutted city
that resulted from such reforms? Would the bourgeois and the
homeless not both turn up their noses at such a purely functional city?

Those who would liquidate beautiful things to fight poverty
reduce poverty to a purely material phenomenon, and the twentieth century has repeatedly shown that once any human problem is conceived of in merely material terms, slaughter usually follows. Of this tendency, Nicolás Gómez Dávila opines, "A
simple fit of impatience often soon bridges the distance between
utopia and murder." Hence, abortion is typically defended for
economic reasons. If poverty is a perennial human problem, as
Christ says, stripping a city bare to end poverty will not work.
Once a city has been stripped bare, its citizens no longer enjoy
the public beauty which proclaims that every man has a soul and

that love of neighbor is essential to the health of the soul. As opposed to regarding beautiful things as privations of charity, it is more fitting to see them as incarnations of sermons which preach generosity.

Even when fortified by such reasoning, the cathedral which undertakes a fifty-million-dollar-restoration does so in front of the poor who file in to pray. It may be that any cathedral which begins such a project is also simultaneously giving more to charity than the Marxist reading room down the street; however, it is nonetheless true that all fifty million dollars could be given to the poor and their pain could be somewhat alleviated. If the poor are not invited to watch the bishop sign the contract which inaugurates the restoration, it is because beauty is unavoidably embarrassing.

At the same time, it is because the cathedral *is* justifiable that uncommon things cannot be conflated with luxury goods. An Hermès Birkin bag which cost twenty-five thousand dollars has nothing to do with confirming the dignity of all men and everything to do with the exclusive exaltation of the individual. On this point, it is worth noting that the aristocratic system which the French Revolutionaries decried for its inequalities was actually far better at creating equality than the capitalist, consumerist way of life which followed it. Many a young self-made celebrity has, in short order, accumulated a personal net worth which exceeds that of most aristocratic family fortunes. Income disparity is far greater now than it was before the French Revolution, but this is because aristocracies foster stability and longevity while mediocrity creates massive highs, radicalized fervor, and crushing lows.

Cathedrals, Collective Assets, and Commodification

If beautiful things are repositories of generosity that can be perpetually drawn upon, it follows that bad taste is not a morally neutral concern, like a preference for coffee over tea or blue drapes over gray ones. Good taste entails the enjoyment of beauty, which is a gratuity of being, while bad taste is a spiritual malady that cannot help cultivating stinginess. When people prefer things which do not last over things that do, they invariably create chaotic societies where long-term cultural projects are impossible. On a cultural level, ugliness does not follow poverty so much as poverty follows ugliness: bad taste is far, far more expensive than good taste.

Of course, the same people who want to liquidate beautiful things and give the proceeds to the poor also tend to throw their weight behind fashionable projects that aim to change the world. Because things of great beauty last, they impede change. Despite having a positive, vaguely inspirational air, "change the world" is really nothing other than an exhortation to seize power, for newly-seized power invariably creates change. Although the concept of progress entails a destination, progressives cannot agree for long on what this destination should be. For those with short memories, any change gives a convincing impersonation of progress. But for well over a hundred years now, progressives have been unable to convince their children to continue toward the same destinations they have laid out, and so intellectual patricide has become the modus operandi of the Left.

Such intellectual internecine strife compares poorly with the marvelous consistency of medieval Christianity. The fifth-century writings of St. Augustine are easily harmonized with the eleventh-century writings of St. Anselm of Canterbury, though they were separated by hundreds of miles, spoke different languages, and grew up in very different sociopolitical environments. On the other hand, compare fashionable books about gender from the 1960s, the 1990s, and today. A vast array of acrimonious disagreements exists between them. How have Christians been able to maintain so much consistency of thought and purpose for so long?

Consider the Notre Dame cathedral, which took more than eight generations to complete. Those who were involved in its groundbreaking had no expectation of seeing the cathedral finished. This made it easier for the children of the groundbreakers to continue the work of their parents. For the average builder, there was little hope of enjoying the completed cathedral, and thus the project was highly resistant to anyone's selfishness—a cathedral is too massive a project for anyone to bend the entire thing toward his own private gain.

However, as soon as a generation undertakes a project which can be finished in a single lifetime, their children have incentive to scrap that project in favor of ones more suited to their own tastes and values. Any social or cultural project which will take fifty years to accomplish encounters profound existential threats halfway through, for everyone who started the project begins to age out of productivity and those who enter mid-way have both incentive and ability to redirect time and funds to a more fashionable endeavor which does not seem so dated.

As an ideology, then, the problem with "change the world" is that it is too easily accomplished. Change is doable over and over again, and new schemes of change undermine and abolish the changes of a previous generation. Everyone who changes the world is undermining or abolishing the change that some wide-eyed, well-meaning dreamer undertook just a few years ago, for "change the world" always involves crushing the dream of someone slightly older than yourself who wanted to do the same thing. Thus we reach a paradox: unless a society undertakes a project it cannot hope to accomplish, it will not accomplish anything lasting.

Of course, it is impossible to persuade people who do not believe in the soul to undertake a project they will never benefit from. Multigenerational progress requires multigenerational agreement on the destination; otherwise subsequent generations will crisscross the same desert for thousands of years and never arrive at the promised land. Multigenerational agreement requires a willingness to honor mother and father, which is a sticking point for progressives, who invariably regard elders as traitors. As Edmund Burke once said, "People will not look forward to posterity who never look back to their ancestors."[3] Love for our ancestors is difficult, though, for our ancestors are flawed and our posterity is not. Looking to the past means seeking the advice of the elderly, and the elderly never have pleasant advice. Loving posterity is easy so long as posterity remains abstract; once our children reach the age of maturity, loving them becomes far more challenging. Since the French Revolution, each successive generation has believed it has finally arrived at the articulation of a cultural project which their children would respect, but as James Baldwin once said, "Children have never been very good at listening to their elders, but they have never failed to imitate them."[4] Every man who disregards his father teaches his children to do the same. Every young man who claims to stand "on the right side of history" has already begun daring his grandchildren to report him for treason.

This idea is deeply offensive to modern Christians who have, over the past fifty years, pried much of the church's glorious old beauty from the walls, song books, and altar. We have sold our glory to the world at a cut rate, and in return we have received fashionable churches with nightclub names and coffeehouse vibes, churches which mug corporate websites for their creeds and prattle endlessly about community and authenticity, churches which are built on business models that will be obsolete in ten years and inspire cynicism and apostasy in those who hold out long enough to see the doors close for good.

The desire for beautiful things is a matter of both personal and corporate responsibility, for things of great beauty are, as Roger Scruton describes, collective assets much like "peace, freedom, law, civility, public spirit, the security of property and family life, in all of which we depend on the cooperation of others while having no means singlehandedly to obtain them."[5] While a particular recording of Bach's unaccompanied cello suites might belong to the cellist who performed them, more generally speaking, Bach's cello suites are part of a cultural heritage which all men share the responsibility for perpetuating. If no one attended performances of Bach's cello suites, the music could easily become lost in the shuffle of history. Similarly, visiting museums is a corporate responsibility, for a museum is only open today because patrons came last year.

This is not to say that particular persons cannot be the legal owners of particular works of art or that it is immoral for those persons to profit from that ownership, for many of the great works that have been created throughout history are the product of the relationship between an artist and a wealthy patron.

Nonetheless, the money with which wealthy patrons subsidized the arts ultimately came from common people. The cultural artifacts created from such an arrangement did not need to turn a profit, which means the artist was free to make his music, his painting, or his poetry, as good or beautiful as he could. Good things are rare, and good things endure because people who care about goodness seek them out generation after generation. It is through this generational interest that something becomes "a classic," and responsibility for its perpetuation is diffusely shared by society at large. In this way, patronized art is a gift which society comes to collectively possess. Once very good things are evaluated and appreciated as collective assets, it behooves us to ask whether a society tends toward the creation and preservation of beautiful things or whether it aims only to amuse itself.

Under a system of patronage, one could imagine someone arguing that the public should decide for themselves what art they wanted to be patronized, for surely they would demand something of the highest quality. While history has proven all such generous assessments of the public to be laughable, we can appreciate the apparent common sense of a system wherein art is reimagined as a commodity which must appeal to a broad range of people and not just a privileged class. Would music and literature created to please the public not be more universal and thus more human?

And yet, one must also recall the legendary story of Lycurgus, who, when asked by certain men to establish a democracy, replied, "Begin with your own family." Were a family of six to decide the week's dinner menu with a popular vote, the family would eat burgers and fries every night until they all collapsed dead of heart disease. It is the task of the mother and father to see the matter of diet from an enlarged perspective. They must observe the world long enough to know what becomes of those who only eat food which is very tasty, although the children cannot turn their eyes from the tremendous pleasure set before them. One need only listen to a Top Forty radio station for half an hour to know that children now determine the musical menu from which all Americans must eat, whether or not they wish to, for popular music is omnipresent and plays constantly at department stores, grocery stores, and sporting events, not to mention during commercials, films, and Sunday worship at most American churches.

In the end, the commodification of art has failed to produce more humane music and literature because it has created a system wherein no one can be held responsible for the pap and twaddle presented to the public for consumption. Within a system of commodified art, if a certain film is profitable, more films like it will be made, even if the film is poorly reviewed and audiences do not like it. The man who purchases a ticket for a mindless blockbuster might tell himself that this is nothing more than a lark, or that he will balance out this vapid entertainment by reading a thousand lines in *Paradise Lost*, or that he is a cool observer of human nature who occasionally puts his finger to the pulse of society just so he can shake his head sadly at the weak heartbeat he feels. And yet, none of these reasons register at the box office. The box office makes no distinction between an enthusiastic purchase and a despondent, ironic one. In paying for a movie ticket, a man registers a ten-dollar vote in favor of more of the same. Neither the employees of the theater nor the film's distributors care if moviegoers think that a film is good, and neither does the modern moviegoer feel a sense of ownership or moral culpability for the art he patronizes. The modern man does not regard the purchase of art as an activity with ethical connotations: his responsibility for the films he watches, the records he streams, and the books he buys is so diffusely spread out among tens of millions of other people that he feels his choices do not ultimately matter. One ticket more or less will not change anything on a cultural level, and neither will viewing one more blockbuster matter much to his soul.

Under a system of patronage, someone in particular had to take responsibility for the goodness (or badness) of a piece of art. Blame could not be endlessly shifted back and forth between the undiscerning public, exhibitionist performers, and greedy promoters, as responsibility for a work of art was squarely placed on the creator and the patron. However, without anyone in particular to blame for the proliferation of bad art, society lost the ability to say that "bad art" even existed. Aesthetic relativism is less a principled philosophical stance than a reflection on the consumerist system which now produces art.

Any society which abandons traditional standards of goodness and badness, beauty and ugliness, loses a compelling reason to keep any particular cultural artifact or creed around. Thus our interest in new songs, new films, new books, and new political causes rises quickly and falls even more quickly. If we believe that these new songs and films are good and beautiful and true, we cannot also believe that goodness and beauty and truth are transcendent, because transcendent things last and pop culture doesn't. If we do *not* believe that the songs and films and causes which grab our interest are good and beautiful and true, then we must admit there is some other reason why we seek them out. Before the French Revolution, men sought out truth, beauty, and

goodness because they believed these things brought them nearer to God: man was terrified of his passing and fragile nature
and he feared nonexistence, so he sought to join himself with
the immortal God that he might draft on God's transcendence.
In abandoning God, modernity likewise abandoned transcendence. We still have gods, but they are imminent. They are here
and now and nowhere else in the past or the future.

Imminent gods require a culture of immanence, and so we
have exalted art which affects us immediately and intensely,
playing to our appetites and not our intellects. Most popular art
is easy to like and easy to understand, offering an experience that
is sleek, sensual, sexy, shocking, spectacular, loud, flashy, funny,
or frenetic. By contrast, art which is subtle, paradoxical, and nuanced is now thought heretical because it requires long periods
of contemplation, and by the time it is understood, we will have
moved on to the worship of new gods. This is the great difference between commodified art and patronized art. Commodified art requires no struggle, for it has been created to suit our
tastes. But patronized art does not exist to please us; rather, it
calls us to make ourselves worthy of it.

It is tempting to say that the books we choose to read and the
music we choose to listen to is "all a matter of personal taste,"
and yet an affinity for old things has taken on a nearly religious
weight: the man who would be faithful to things which last must
now be willing to stomach charges of blasphemy.

Endnotes

1. David Bentley Hart, *The Beauty of the Infinite* (Grand Rapids: Eerdmans, 2004), 16.

2. Roger Scruton, *A Very Short Introduction to Beauty* (Oxford: Oxford University Press, 2009), 3.

3. Edmund Burke, *Reflections on the Revolution in France*, Reissue (Oxford: Oxford University Press (2009), 33.)

4. James Baldwin, *Nobody Knows My Name*, Reissue (New York: Vintage, 1992), 62.

5. Roger Scruton, *How to be a Conservative* (London: Bloomsbury Academic, 2014), viii.

7.

On Nature

"O Lord, how lovely it is to be Thy guest: breeze full of scents; mountains reaching to the skies; waters like boundless mirrors, reflecting the sun's golden rays and the scudding clouds."
—From the Akathist of Thanksgiving

In chapter four, I suggested there is something "special" about art of the twentieth century which makes it unusually easy to identify even for those who are uneducated in art history. In the same way that I have sketched out a very particular definition of the word *mediocre*, I would like to do the same for *special*.

To begin with, the existence of special things presumes the existence of common things. To say a thing is special is to say it is set apart, and what are special things set apart from if not non-special things? A certain movie cannot be special unless there are non-special movies. A song cannot be special without a host of average songs or normal songs that fail to distinguish themselves. Scripture acknowledges that there are common things and special things, though the authors of Scripture never use the word "special." Instead, they speak of "holy" or "sacred" things. Generally speaking, God does not create things that are holy from the start. He creates things that are common, then sets them apart later through ceremonies and rituals which confer holiness upon them.

Although every culture in the history of mankind has acknowledged the difference between common and holy things, the Christian concept of holiness is unusual when compared to pagan understandings. Pagans believed that holy things were set apart for their gods, but they did not believe their gods were omnipresent. Pagans knew their gods were finite, limited, circumscribable, and thus a certain plant, animal, or grove of trees was sacred to a god because the god resided therein. Pagan gods maintained transactional relationships with their devotees, just like modern governments have transactional relationships with citizens. The citizens of Richmond, Virginia, pay taxes to the Richmond government, and the Richmond government provides service to the citizens by way of those taxes. The citizens of Albany, New York, do not pay taxes to the city of Richmond, but the Richmond mayor doesn't mind, and neither does the Richmond city council. The citizens of Albany pay taxes to a different city government, and that government, in turn, takes care of them. In the same manner, pagan gods were territorial. Apollo protected the people who offered him sacrifices, and the same was true of Athena, Baal, and so forth. The people of Baal were untroubled that foreign nations did not offer sacrifices to Baal, for neither did Baal provide those nations with health and safety.

The territorial quality of the gods meant that pagans believed in a hard line which separated common things from holy things, or natural things from supernatural things. I often summarize the pagan concept of holiness for my students with just three words: *here, not there.* Just as the gods were local, so was holiness local. A certain flower was holy because it sustained the presence of a god, and yet this same god was absent from other flowers and so those things were common.

Christians, on the other hand, acknowledge a difference between the natural and the supernatural but do not believe that a hard line separates those two realms. Unlike the pagan gods, the Triune God is "at all times, and in all places, filling all things," according to the Prayer to the Holy Spirit (an ancient Orthodox Prayer) which also means Christians do not believe that holiness is a localized phenomenon. Instead, Christians believe a thing becomes holy when God manifests Himself through that thing, though He was already present. When a thing becomes holy, it is not because God has suddenly arrived to take up residence in that thing. Rather, holiness is simply the finite, temporal manifestation of God's omnipresence.

Within Christian thought, then, the common and the holy are not at war. The natural is eternally pregnant with the supernatural, always ready to give birth to divine knowledge. So, while Christians acknowledge holy books (Scripture), holy baths (baptism), holy days (Christmas), holy relationships (marriage), and holy food (communion), Scripture also depicts God suddenly revealing Himself in gushing rocks, burning bushes, and even the shadows of the apostles. God vouchsafes to meet man in traditional ways and predictable places, but He may meet us wherever and whenever He chooses. Even when God does not personally, explicitly reveal Himself in nature (as he did with Moses), nature is yet His handiwork and reveals His character in subtle ways. Nature and supernature are not opposites, neither are secular things at odds with sacred things, and so Christians have no complaint with nature or with common things. Man was made a little lower than the angels, and the lesser glory of the earth is perfectly suited to him.

Thus, when progressives and Christians speak of "nature," they are not referring to the same thing. Within the framework of Christian thought, nature can only be understood in its relationship with the supernatural. In the same way, a husband can only be understood in his relationship with a wife. Apart from a wife, apart from a marriage, the concept of "husband" is meaningless. Were someone to suggest that "husband" was simply a feeling or a habit and that small children, single men, and old women could suddenly become husbands just as easily as they could become angry or become smokers, this use of the word "husband" would not be a nuanced variation of the word's traditional meaning but rather a complete rejection. Were the concept of "husband" defined apart from marriage, it would become meaningless and contemptible, for it would simply be a title which someone assumed for himself (or herself, or her dog) apropos of nothing. If someone could, from a resting position, transform himself into a husband through sheer willpower, husbands could not be terribly important to the world. After all, if becoming a husband were based on desire alone, why would society need them or even want them around? What useful service could they offer? If the concept of "husband" is not attached to any observable phenomenon or set of standards, the so-called husband exists merely for his or her own amusement. If husbands are not obligated to do anything, then there is no such thing as a good husband or a bad husband, and husbands do not matter. Any mode of being which is entirely divorced from duty is superfluous.

Similarly, in cutting off nature from supernature, the Enlightenment inaugurated a long, slowly unfurling contempt for both which reaches new heights every year. The effect is somewhat ironic, as no Enlightenment philosopher or French Revolutionary would have said they despised nature—they claimed the opposite, in fact, and saw themselves as liberating it from the irrational magic, superstition, and hocus pocus of the supernatural. Since the hundred years following the Reformation had handily proved that religion was given to ambiguity and dispute, the secularists believed that by disencumbering nature from Christianity, they could enable real progress in science and technology.

What Usually Happens

Before going further, though, I must give a little shape to what I mean by "nature," which is a notoriously slippery concept. A definition of nature may lean toward the theological, with nature as an intermediary between the human and the divine, an unbiased judge of right and wrong that can be appealed to when man believes he has been treated unfairly by God. Or, nature may refer to what is, or what ought to be, each of which requires a nuanced metaphysical explanation. However, I would like to define "nature" in a simple manner which throws traditionalist and progressive differences into high relief: nature is *what usually happens.*

This definition suits a discussion of human nature and Mother Nature alike. Whether a man is concerned with kings, paupers, plants, pandas, minerals, models, math, production, propulsion, or prostitutes, when he learns what usually happens—what usually works, what usually hurts, what is usually said, what is usually felt—a man has discovered something about that thing's nature. When a man learns that holding very hot things is usually painful, he learns something about his fleshly nature. When a boy learns that lying to his mother usually leads to fear and remorse, he learns something about his spiritual nature. When we observe that dogs usually become ill after eating chocolate, we learn something about canine nature. Tendency and propensity invariably teach us about nature.

Accordingly, if a man wants to understand nature—especially his own nature (be it his human nature, his masculine nature, his adult nature, his middle-class nature, his Catholic nature)— he must be willing to admit what usually happens. What usually becomes of Catholics who quit going to church? What usually becomes of men who start drinking before lunch? What usually becomes of adults who quit exercising? If a man despises nature, he will not fear getting drunk in the morning, regardless of what he has seen such a practice do to other men. If he despises nature, he will not fear giving up church attendance or exercise or bringing his wife flowers on Friday afternoon. But on what grounds would a man expect his own behavior to pan out differently than the exact same behavior usually pans out in the lives of men just like himself? On the grounds that he is "special."

"Special" always entails an exception from what is usual, an exception from nature. Why would anyone want an exception from nature, though?

A thing's nature is an invisible, interior blueprint which subtly instructs and inclines it toward happiness, unity, long life, and flourishing. In some sense, a man *is* his nature. However, because every man possesses a soul, this means that he has both a natural and a supernatural aspect. Because animals lack a supernatural aspect, they cannot fight their natures. A certain dog might make for a lousy pet, but no dog makes for a lousy dog, at least not in the same way that some human beings make for lousy human beings. Because animals are not contemplative creatures, they do not consider the past or the future, but act on instinct, which is only a little malleable. A human being, on the other hand, can submit his natural aspect to his supernatural aspect (becoming a "spiritual man," as St. Paul says in 2 Corinthians 2:15), or he can use his supernatural aspect to make war on his nature (becoming a "carnal man").

Like all blueprints, though, nature imposes limitations on human life, and men have a curious and unexplainable history of fighting these limitations, to their own embarrassment and pain. The Roman poet Horace once said, "You may drive out nature with a pitchfork, but she keeps coming back,"[1] a proverb which rings true for every man who regularly falls prey to a particular temptation, chastises himself for not recalling the shame which attended his last failure, makes many oaths to not fall prey to temptation again, and then inexplicably does so just a few hours later.

While reasonable people have known for many thousands of years that nature cannot be bested, modern men are unusually squeamish when it comes to discussing what usually happens to people who eat too much, or what usually becomes of children who are given too much praise, or what usually happens to boys whose fathers travel too much. We hope that the standards do not apply to us, that our exceptions will hold out, and that no one will notice the small ways in which we are breaking the rules. The great hope of modern man is to cheat nature.

Nature and Politics

When Enlightened philosophers considered what kind of government they believed to be most suitable to mankind, they were unwilling to believe that humanity existed from its origins in a relationship with God. Monarchical theorists claimed government was not human in origin, but divine—after all, God arranged his angels hierarchically and ordained the stars to govern "sacred times, and days and years" (Gen. 1:14). Adam and Eve inherited their power from God, and God's power was kingly, not democratic. Together, King Adam and Queen Eve were commanded to rule a great kingdom which God had carefully established before handing them the keys. Adam and Eve did not invent rule. They stepped into a vast river of rule which extended back much further than they could possibly see.

The divine right of kings was challenged by Enlightenment philosophers, who were skeptical about the literal interpretation of Scripture. When he laid out his theory of governance in *The Social Contract* in 1762, the philosopher Jean-Jacques Rousseau posited that government could not be stably built upon myth, the interpretation of which was contentious and often disputed. Scripture could be used as a guide for personal morality and private devotion, but civic peace should not be staked upon it, for the interpretation of Scripture led to numerous disagreements. Rather, civic peace and law should be based purely on reason. Under this conception, government became an entirely human endeavor. But if government was originally instituted by man, there must have been some point at which it did not exist. And if there was a point when government did not exist, Rousseau asked, why did human beings first decide to create it? If there was a time when all men did as they pleased, what caused men to give up that freedom and create laws which limited their abilities?

Rousseau argued that man originally formed government for his own "advantage."[2] He speculated that prior to the formation of the first government, men lived near one another but maintained total independence. When a number of closely-clustered autonomous individuals were threatened by invasion, plague, drought, or some other natural disaster, they decided that the benefits of union outweighed the dangers of lonely self-determination and consented to obey certain collectively determined laws. (In considering this speculation, it ought to be noted that Rousseau's ideas are entirely theoretical and that no evidence exists which confirms such a scenario has ever existed in history. Nonetheless, when I tell my students that no evidence exists for Rousseau's claims, there is always someone who objects, "What about cave drawings?" When I ask them to explain, they launch into various uncritical assumptions in which very old depictions of hunters and animals on cave walls somehow prove that cavemen, as they are popularly understood, used to exist, that they all violently fended for themselves, and that they determined to create society from scratch at some point. As marvelous as I find the caves of Lascaux to be, they are not, in and of themselves, a justification for Enlightenment theories of government.)

The upshot of Rousseau's reasoning was that government exists primarily to curb human suffering and satisfy human desires. He did not conceive of government as a transcendent enterprise, for an Enlightened government must necessarily change as often as human desires change. If government exists to make men happy, one can think of society as a game wherein the rules can be endlessly manipulated for the pleasure of the players. If four people sitting down to play Monopoly agree to begin the game with five hundred dollars, it is done. The players need not conjure the ghost of Lizzie Magie, the creator of the game, and obtain her permission to alter the rules. Neither do the four players need to petition Parker Brothers, the publisher of the game, for the right to edit the rules. And should the four players all be underage, it is ludicrous to think they need consent from the owner of the house wherein they are playing just to customize the rules. Provided that all the players agree, the game can happily and justly proceed.

According to Rousseau, the same was true in a democracy, for just as a game exists for the pleasure of the players, so does government exist for the pleasure of citizens. As soon as government exists for any other reason than the pleasure of citizens, it has become exploitative. Rousseau thought of laws in terms of desire, not obligation—as soon as people are obligated to a power outside themselves, religious acrimony quickly follows, for diverse societies cannot agree on which outside power should be obeyed. When it comes to whose desires are upheld when making laws, it is a matter of timing: past generations had their chance, future generations will get theirs. The only people who really matter, at least so far as the game goes, are those presently situated around the table.

Consequently, the Enlightenment reoriented man in time.

Behind or Before?

For millennia, Western man believed that the past was in front of him and the future was behind him. With his face toward the past, he cautiously walked backwards into the future. For this reason, prior to the Enlightenment, cultural change took place very slowly. As I noted earlier, the theology of St. Augustine is largely consistent with the theology of St. Anselm of Canterbury, even though they were separated by many centuries and many hundreds of miles. Whence came this consistency? Despite their economic and regional differences, we could say that Augustine and Anselm grew up in the same city and even in the same house because they trained their gaze on many of the same things. Both men thought that the future was unknowable and uncontrollable and were oriented toward the past, believing that ancient poets and philosophers bore witness to inescapable truths about human nature. Neither thought of the past as a thing which could be escaped, for inasmuch as the past revealed human nature, the past revealed the future, as well.

When explaining this older view of man's orientation in time to my students, I ask them to imagine a man walking backwards along an unfamiliar mountain path. He moves slowly because he does not know what is behind him and there may be a snake, a ravine, or a fallen tree branch to avoid. Within the analogy, the present exists on the periphery of the man's vision. The present comes into view slowly, even as the past is always laid out for consideration. Some events in the present can be understood immediately, but others require time and space before they become clear.

If it seems strange to think men ever believed the future was behind them and the past before them, take a moment to consider the unchangeable fixedness of the past and the ultimate uncertainty of the future. The past does not move. It sits patiently still for us so we can examine it, and in doing so we come to know how and why things usually happen. The study of the past is the study of human limitation, but when man is oriented toward the future, he no longer has a fixed world to study and so he can no longer say what will usually happen. Because they face the past and meditate perpetually on the frailty of the world, conservatives are primarily interested in *what has worked*, even if they have suspicions about how things might be changed to work better. Because progressives face the future, they are interested in *what might work better*, even if the search for a better future entails burning their inheritance and scrapping the relative stability and happiness of the present.

The progressive orientation toward the future also entails great optimism. In the future, there is not yet any sin—no act of debauchery or wickedness has yet occurred, no child has yet been abused, no bomb has yet been dropped, and no wars have yet been declared. On the other hand, conservatives are oriented toward the past, where numberless acts of evil have occurred. When faced with the sheer quantity of vice, corruption, death, and depravity in human history, the conservative is impressed that anything at all has lasted. If a man can find something—anything—that lasts, he must hold on to it with all his might.

Monarchy is only a viable form of government among people who believe that man is oriented towards the past. The power of a monarchy is drawn from the past, drawn from tradition, and thus drawn from a consideration of and respect for nature. No king may safely disparage his lineage without daring his people to rebellion. If a king does not respect his past, the people will not respect the king, for the past is the source of the king's power. If the people come to believe that man is existentially oriented toward the future, however, they will quickly tire of the king's orders, for the source of his power will be obsolete.

Some readers may feel the loss of monarchical forms of government to be no great tragedy; however, believing that man is oriented toward the future also invariably leads to a loss of respect for nature. Respect for nature is predicated on man's orientation toward the past, for nature is what usually happens, and knowledge of nature is born of knowing what has already happened. But Enlightenment philosophers claimed that the future is in front of us and that every man is free to choose any point on the horizon and to run toward it as fast as he can—where he finally arrives depends entirely on his own preference. For this reason, the rate of cultural change has dramatically accelerated since the French Revolution, for our wills are endlessly fickle. Before the Enlightenment, man understood that nature imposed limits on his will and that fighting these limitations would always prove a losing battle (the desire to grow swan wings, say, was senseless). After the Enlightenment, though, man came to believe that his will had the power to coerce his nature into doing whatever he wanted.

Within Rousseau's theory of governance, no man could be justly required to obey a law he had not consented to. While he may have meant that only non-consensual political laws need not be obeyed, Rousseau's followers and their great-grandchildren finally came to believe that even unwanted natural laws should be disregarded. Having rejected the idea that natural laws are inviolable, modern men finally came to believe there is no such thing as human nature. If there *was* such a thing as human nature—a hidden, invisible blueprint that every human being must follow in order to be happy—it would be entirely indifferent to our desires. To this day, anyone who describes the inviolable limitations which nature imposes on the will is thought mean-spirited.

When men want things which their natures rebel against, they suffer. But as opposed to quitting the unnatural things which lead to psychic and physical pain, scientists have invented drugs which enable us to continue destroying ourselves painlessly. These drugs drive a deep wedge between our bodies and our souls in an attempt to keep the pain we undergo from reaching the place where true suffering takes place: the soul. Death is the separation of body and soul; however, because modern men no longer believe in nature, they have lost the ability to truly describe what death is, and so life and death are slowly conflated into the same twisted phenomenon. A culture of death cannot fail to grow up wherever nature is rejected.

Having declared nature an oppressive farce and supernature a delusion, Enlightenment sympathizers were forced to create a new category of being with which to describe desirable things. In the old schema, heaven stood above earth and hell was below. Heaven was a higher, better realm which beckoned the earth to rise and enjoy fulfillment in God. The things of man were situated in an existential middle ground between heaven and hell, between the supernatural and the unnatural. Every proper use of nature tended toward heaven, while the abuse, perversion, and exploitation of nature tended toward hell. The middle ground between heaven and hell was not thought neutral, but good, albeit a lesser good than heaven. Virtue always involved the lesser good yielding to the greater good, while vice demanded the opposite.

However, without belief in the supernatural, it has become very difficult to distinguish the natural from the unnatural.

Without the orientation provided by heaven, what is the difference between hell and earth? Without God, how can you distinguish between the human and the demonic? More than two
hundred years after the French Revolution, the only people who
attack a position or practice as "unnatural" are those who believe
in God, because the concept of nature only makes sense as an
intermediary between the supernatural and the unnatural. God
is the Nature of nature. Without God, nature withers and dies,
just as a body withers and dies when cut off from the spirit.

Progressives aptly intuited this, though. They understood
that without God, nature was a dead end. For this reason, a new
category of being was needed which could replace both the supernatural and the natural.

Holiness, but Better

Since the Enlightenment, "special" has slowly taken the place of
"holy." It has become not only a higher form of being but the only
acceptable form of being. "Special" has come to dominate what
Western people want from life—and not just progressives, but
Christians, as well. As a high school teacher, I regularly speak
with parents who tell me that their children are special. Christian lifestyle charlatans have grown wealthy selling books about
how to have a special marriage. Pinterest and Instagram thrive
because we want to throw our children special birthday parties
and persuade our friends that we eat special food and vacation
in special places. Why did pornography become the preeminent
and most prolific modern art form? Because men believed sex
ought to be a special experience.

Simple logic tells us that if some days *are* special, others are not. If some places are special, others are not. If some children are special, others are not. Thanks to a lifetime of indoctrination, however, this is incredibly difficult for us to accept. Very few parents are willing to admit that their children are not special. Were a pastor to tell his parish that his relationship with his wife was "just a run-of-the-mill, garden-variety sort of marriage," many congregants would wonder aloud if he was qualified to give spiritual counsel. Nothing is marketed as average or common. Our world is a highly competitive marketplace of ideas, people, and products, and in such a marketplace, to say a thing is "common" is to admit it is a failure.

As a category of being, "special" is really the opposite of "holy." Because holiness shares in the boundless nature of God, there is always more holiness to go around. Holy things beget holy things: holy water consecrates what it touches, holy places confer their holiness on the activities that transpire therein, holy men confer their holiness on others. But special things cannot confer their specialness on other things. Holiness is an open system, which means that a holy thing can make a common thing holy without losing its own holiness. Specialness is a closed and vampiric system, for one thing cannot become special without devouring or absorbing the specialness of another. The goal of a new blockbuster is to make old blockbusters look dull by comparison. The goal of new clothing styles is to make old clothing styles look dowdy by comparison. The goal of a fashionable new church is to make old churches seem dull and conventional by comparison. The goal of new pornography is to make old pornography look chaste by comparison. The goal of the latest KFC sandwich is to make the last KFC sandwich seem flavorless by comparison.

Avant-garde art and progressive hermeneutics co-opt many aspects of holiness, and yet the aspects of holiness which they reject are far more telling. Within a traditional Christian economy of being, the process whereby common things become holy typically involves some ceremony or ritual: consider a priest performing a wedding, the consecration of bread and wine for communion, God's "hallowing" of the Sabbath. So, too, a common day borrows its holiness from a holy event which takes place thereon: the holiness of December 25th drafts on the holiness of Christ's birth, the holiness of January 6th drafts on the holiness of Christ's baptism, the holiness of March 25th drafts on the holiness of Christ's conception. The holiness of holy things is borrowed from other holy things which, in turn, borrow their holiness from older, higher, or holier things.

By contrast, the specialness of special things is self-derived, which is why special things are perpetually involved in a turf battle with one another. For this reason, we now speak of the box office as a sort of battleground, and modern Americans are just as interested in how much money a new film makes as they are in the story the film tells. In the same way that ancient Romans did not care whether Jupiter was good, contemporary Americans do not care whether wildly popular things are good. Part of the thrill in attending the premiere of a blockbuster franchise film is the knowledge that so many different kinds of people are simultaneously seeing the same movie across the country. The appeal of Christianity cuts across races, income levels, education levels, and political affiliations, but an Avengers film possesses the same sort of universal appeal, and so the individual moviegoer may console himself against feelings of loneliness, alienation, and insignificance by assuring himself that by participating in such cinematic events he is "part of something very big."

Because new special things empty old special things of their specialness, there is no tradition of special and special things end up being short-lived by their very nature. Tradition implies obedience and predictability, but the very specialness of special things is derived from their refusal to obey. Consequently, a thing that is special cannot be refined, tinkered with, tempered, or adjusted the way a traditional form can. Take the splatter paintings of Jackson Pollock, for example. Pollock is famous for being the first person to paint in such a manner; however, he did not inaugurate a new form of painting, for anyone attempting to create drip paintings after Pollock will be accused of thievery, dullness of wit, and a lack of originality. Rather, Pollock claimed a style and content of painting entirely for himself, in much the same way that middle school boys greedily claim slices of pizza by licking them so others will be ashamed to eat them.

The same is true of Mark Rothko's floating rectangles, Barnett Newman's vertical "zip" paintings, Piet Mondrian's intermittently colorful geometry, Franz Kline's thick black lines, or Willem de Kooning's scrawled gobbledygook. None of these painters was interested in nature. Each appealed entirely to the intellect, which is why their work is so easy to describe. In a certain sense, the *Mona Lisa* could be described as "a painting of a brunette with her hands folded," but anyone who has seen the painting would dismiss such a simple description as wildly insufficient. On the other hand, to say that Mark Rothko painted "colorful rectangles" really does sum up the man's oeuvre. The thrill of Rothko's work is entirely bound up in the massive size of his canvases, and the same is true of Pollock and Newman. Had any of them been forced to use notebook-sized canvases, all their power would be lost. On the other hand, the *Mona Lisa* is still interesting when reduced to the size of a postage stamp.

Anyone looking to follow in the footsteps of Pollock, Rothko, or Mondrian is out of luck. Pollock was not interested in painting nature. He was not interested in the world or in reality itself. Rather, he painted himself, as all modern artists must do. In the world of contemporary art, imitation is a failure of self-expression. Imitation is treason, for every act of imitation looks to the past. Imitation also implies hierarchy, for a man must choose whom to imitate. If he aims to imitate no one, however, he may claim success in all that he undertakes, for he has no standard outside himself by which his work can be judged.

Modern Reading Strategies

Within the realm of literature, the ascendance of "special" has also led to profound loneliness, albeit in a somewhat different manner than modern art. Conversations around literature now center on "understanding the experiences of."

The Grapes of Wrath is commonly taught as a book which helps readers understand the experience of the poor. *Narrative of the Life of Frederick Douglass* is a book which helps readers understand the experiences of a slave in the American South. Grace Paley's short stories help us understand the immigrant experience. While apparently straightforward, the expression needs a nuanced explanation.

"Understanding the experiences of . . ." is now a euphemism for coming to feel sympathy for the kind of person who has written a book; however, progressives have also become profoundly critical of the idea that one kind of person may identify his or her own struggles with those of a different kind of person. The postmodern reader regards every inequality in power as an unbridgeable chasm, and no two human beings are empowered in the same way and to the same degree. This has become finely nuanced, with the similarity of the experiences of, say, a twentieth-century Ukrainian immigrant and a nineteenth-century Irish immigrant called into question. Since everyone is empowered differently, the modern reader is inevitably discouraged from finding himself in the experiences of others who don't share his privilege, race, or background. A white man's attempt to see his own struggles in the story of a black man is seen as a kind of trespass or thievery, just as anyone painting drips after Pollock is a thief. Rather, the modern reader should let the experiences of others stand alone as wholly unique and unrepeatable. Every kind of person—nineteenth-century farm laborers, twentieth-century Arab women, twenty-first-century gay Africans—is special, entirely unlike any other kind of person, and thus existentially marooned on an island to which no outsider may visit and from which no native may depart.

And yet, is it fair to assume that the reader who understands the experiences of a certain author or character will necessarily feel sympathy? Is it not possible for an author to sometimes deserve our sympathy, but not always? Do not some readers come to despise certain authors or characters? And by what standard do we judge some authorial intentions as noble and other intentions as wicked? And if it is possible to read two books and feel sympathy for one author but not another, how do we discern who is worthy of sympathy and who is not?

The modern desire to "understand the experiences of . . ." is not ultimately about distinguishing right from wrong, goodness from badness, or ugliness from beauty, but simply marveling at otherness. This leaves modern readers bereft of tools with which to condemn evil, the text itself stripped of any force, and power resting entirely in the hands of the person choosing which books will be read. If the highest aspiration of the reader is to understand the experiences of the author, then Adolf Hitler's *Mein Kampf* and Stefan Zweig's *The Post-Office Girl* have the same moral and literary value, even though the former author was a monster who terrified and oppressed the latter author, who was a delicate observer of the human condition. But if "understanding the experiences of . . ." is a mode of reading which is incompatible with *Mein Kampf,* then where is the line which divides men whose experiences are worth understanding from men whose experiences are worthless? It is only through standards which transcend experience that monsters may be condemned as monsters.

When one considers modern reading strategies and the interpretation of avant-garde art, a host of similarities emerge between holiness and the modern notion of specialness. Like the oracles of Pythia or the bizarre visions of St. John, Rothko's rectangles and Pollock's drips may only be interpreted by priest-like figures who make the meaning of the paintings (somewhat) knowable to the uninitiated. A young child and an old man might be similarly moved by a painstakingly rendered painting of the crucified Christ, but the banal simplicity of Rothko's work can only be completely understood by a trained scholar who may need tens of thousands of words to explain why, despite all appearances, a few shapes on a canvas are actually brilliant. Like desert-dwelling ascetics who can intuitively decipher a man's whole life in the lines of his face, interpreters of avant-garde paintings see beyond the surface and delve directly into the spirit. But even though vetted "clergy" may speak with authority on the meaning of Rothko's work, every layman is also permitted a private interpretation, provided that the interpretation avers the authentic genius of the work. And since no affirming or appreciative interpretation can be wrong, avant-garde work generously affirms the viewer's special hypothesis about it.

Similarly, when the highest aspiration of the reader is to understand the experiences of the author, the author assumes divine authority over the reader for he is beyond criticism. At the same time, the specialness of the author also places him outside the range of the audience's understanding, for the act of understanding entails reconciling foreign concepts or experiences to familiar ones. This is difficult to allow when a progressive reader is unwilling to admit that the experiences of unempowered people have anything to do with the experiences of empowered ones. No progressive heterosexual would claim, "I understand Tony Kushner's *Angels in America*," because understanding implies equality, nearness. One kind of person may only engage with the art of a different kind of person in order to proclaim, "I can't understand it, but that's okay."

For this reason, not even an "empowered" author is thought to be truly right, for what is right can be understood by others—and if the empowered author is right, he subscribes to a transcendent standard. Rather than being truthful, then, the author becomes Truth itself. Everything the empowered author says boils down to *I am*, for his identity, his argument, his struggle, and his strength are all interchangeable. The modern author is not a human being but an impassable god. In the same way that God's thoughts are higher than man's thoughts, so the author's experiences are higher than the reader's experiences. In the same way that God does not dwell in temples made with hands "as though He needed anything," the modern author does not need anything from the modern reader. "No man has seen God at any time," says St. John, and no one has truly understood the modern author. His power is his unknowability.

A New Twist on an Old Favorite

From the self-derived authority of the avant-garde artist to the unknowability of the modern author to the universal appeal of the blockbuster film, special things both ape holiness and impiously pilfer the aesthetics of the sacred. But in addressing the corrupt specialness of avant-garde artists and progressives, I risk lulling conservative readers into a false sense of security. Specialness is by no means the exclusive interest of college English departments, modern art museums, and movie theaters. While I regularly distinguish between progressive thought and Christian thought, the fact is that most modern Christians reason like progressives because we have absorbed the progressive notion that the past is behind us, and the whole length and breadth of progressive thought flows rather naturally out of that single premise. Many American Christians exhibit contempt for holiness by turning up their noses at the long-standing traditions and conventions of the church in favor of "special" versions of the same. A good number of churches advertise that they are different and "not like other churches," although their websites seem perfectly interchangeable with others making the same claim. Traditional wedding services are modified to suit contemporary fashions and the unique tastes of the bride and groom, who do not want the image of the church impressed on their union, preferring that their own image be impressed on the church. The problem is not that a twenty-first-century wedding service is different from a nineteenth-century wedding service, for some degree of evolution is natural and cannot be helped: the problem is that Christian society has come to expect something striking, original, and unique about every wedding. The traditional aspects of weddings, funerals, and worship services are thought insipid, dull, and uninspired in a way that only novelty and spectacle can rescue. Special churches conduct special weddings, which in turn lead to special marriages, and special marriages simply don't last.

Because specialness is self-derived and not borrowed from a transcendent power, it tends to crumble under the pressure of time. Specialness is a terrible burden which very few things are strong enough to shoulder for very long. Just as the dazzling mechanical toys in Margery Williams' *The Velveteen Rabbit* quickly fall apart, so do dazzling movies and songs. In her classic children's book, Williams distinguishes between two kinds of toys: plain toys which last and special toys which do not. The special toys are characterized as "having things that buzz inside" and "a stick-out handle,"[3] while the plain toys are full of sawdust. The special toys are enjoyed for what they do, while the plain toys are loved for what they are. A teddy bear with one arm is just as good as a teddy bear with two, but once the little mechanisms and springs inside the special toys quit working, they are useless—it rarely makes sense to fix special things, for they are not made to last and can usually be replaced as simply as they can be repaired. Because they have no spiritual value, we feel little shame at throwing them away. Special toys are less interesting over time not only because they fall apart but also because their use is so limited: a mechanical teddy bear can only say a few words, but a stuffed teddy bear can say anything, for a child's imagination intervenes and speaks on behalf of the bear.

In the same way that Teddy Ruxpin was marketed as a better version of the plain teddy bear, special things are presented as an antidote to the ordinary, as sacraments of specialness which alleviate the boredom and meaninglessness induced by everything common. They cannot be presented as holy in an outright way, for holiness pertains to the soul and conjures thoughts of quietude, eternity, stillness, judgment, morality, piety, and contemplation, which are not thoughts which entice spending money. But if a mediocre thing is marketed as "special," it can be set apart from common things without invoking any sort of spiritual blessing or ceremony.

"Special" is nothing more than fake holiness.

Endnotes

1. Horace, *Epistles*, I. x. 24.

2. Jean-Jacques Rousseau, *The Social Contract*, trans. Maurice Cranston (London: Penguin Classics, 1968), 51.

3. Marjorie Williams, *The Velveteen Rabbit* (Tarrytown: Marshall Cavendish Corporation, 2011), 12.

8.

On Fakery

"Weak things must boast of being new. . . . But strong things can boast of being old."

—G. K. Chesterton

Having abandoned the concept of nature, modern men have largely lost the ability to judge whether anything is fake. In the same way that special things cannot exist unless there are normal ones, we may not declare anything fake unless we are willing to acknowledge that some things are real. However, "real" is a concept which implies not only the existence of something which transcends mere appearances but a confidence that this something can manifest itself in tangible, material forms.

Consider the difference between a real Chanel handbag and a fake one. Despite its fakeness, the counterfeit handbag is nonetheless a real thing, neither phantasm nor illusion, and it can hold a wallet and keys just as well as a real Chanel handbag. The fact that something is fake does not mean it is devoid of functionality: a fake Rolex can keep time, fake breasts can arouse lust, and fake competence can inspire trust. A rather common means of determining a real from a fake is to examine the details, the aspects of a thing which are only visible up close. Let us suppose that a real Chanel handbag could be identified through forty separate details: color, shape, stitching, the design of the buckles and clips, the fonts used on the tags, and so forth. The fake Chanel handbags that sell for twenty dollars at Battery Park in New York City only approximate a few details of the original. The person who buys a fake Chanel handbag is not concerned whether the font on the interior tags is convincing, though, because the fake is not designed to fool the kind of person who gets close enough to the bag to check its authenticity. Likewise, fake cash does not need to fool an employee of the United States Secret Service, just the cashier of a department store.

These examples are somewhat extreme, for fake designer goods and fake cash demand a greater likeness to the real thing than most fakes do. Generally speaking, fake things take three or four of the most obvious or most pleasant aspects of the real item and blow them out of proportion until none of the esoteric or difficult aspects of the real thing are left.

A friend who worked at a small grocery store once told me about a certain summer day when the season's first crop of fresh watermelons was delivered. The produce manager cut up one of the melons and invited the employees of the store to have a sample. A crowd formed around the fruit, thick slices were handed out, and every employee except one began eating. When they noticed a certain young woman had not taken a slice of watermelon, her coworkers asked her if she wanted one. She declined by saying, "I wouldn't like it." Her claim hung heavily in the air, and then someone asked, "Have you *never* tasted watermelon?"

She replied, "I've tasted watermelon candy." At once, everyone insisted she try the real thing. They told her she would love it—that there was nothing like real watermelon—so she hesitantly accepted an offered slice and took a bite.

When I tell this story to my students, I always break at this point and ask, "What did she think of the watermelon?" The first students to speak say, "She loved it," and then a smaller number of students guess the opposite. They debate the matter for a few minutes, although the students who think that she did not like real watermelon are usually at a loss to explain why.

"She tried the watermelon and did not like it," I finally tell them, "because she didn't think it was sweet enough."

Anyone who has been raised on fake watermelon will find real watermelon bland. Why? Because fake flavors are cartoonishly intense. Plus, real watermelon is not only more expensive than watermelon candy, it also entails a greater hassle. Watermelon candy can be enjoyed cleanly, neatly, and cheaply, while eating a real watermelon involves hauling a twenty-pound fruit from the store to the car, from the car to the house, and then sloppily cutting it up, finding room in the fridge for all the pieces, and cleaning up the knife, the cutting board, and the children after they dribble watermelon juice all over themselves. In the same way, real romance involves courtship, gifts, vows, poems, arguments, apologies, health insurance, confrontation, forgiveness, and the difficult reconciliation of two separate ways of life. Fake romance—either through pornography, prostitution, or fantasy—is cheaper, faster, cleaner, and more discrete. A fake romance reduces a real romance to its most physically pleasant aspects and then disregards everything else.

The easy defense of mediocre food, music, films, and clothes improperly assumes that these things are real and that they exist on the same continuum as good things and great things, merely at a lesser station of glory. However, the difference between a real ten-dollar bill and a fake ten-dollar bill is not like the difference between a sixty-four-inch television and an eighteen-inch television. A counterfeit ten-dollar bill isn't actually worth a dollar and twenty cents: it has no real value and no real goodness. A thing is not real merely because it does something. A counterfeit bill does not become authentic currency just because a cashier accepts it, nor is a counterfeit bill real just because it is made with real green ink and real cotton paper. A fake Chanel bag does not become real just because your phone doesn't fall through the bottom—it is not the handbag-ness of the thing which is fake, but the Chanel-ness. We determine whether a thing is real or fake on the basis of where it comes from. The only real Chanel handbags are those handbags derived from the Chanel company. The only real American dollars are those whose production is sanctioned by the Treasury Department. The only real watermelons are those produced by nature.

Progressives may accept the distinction between real and fake Chanel handbags. However, because progressives view every human as a self-derived and self-determined being, they are not willing to accept a distinction between real and fake men or real and fake women. When no man is beholden to the nature he receives, he comes from himself, creates himself, and may only be held accountable for "being himself." If there is no power higher than the individual, then everyone can determine for himself what is real and reality is no longer the harmonious relationship between the apparent and the transcendent. We are now willing to call just about anything in a skirt "a woman."

If there is anything worth suffering or sacrificing for, there will also be a market for fake versions of that thing. Fake designer goods convey an image of wealth and good taste where there is none. Fake flavors convey a love of nature where there is none. Fake virtues convey an image of selflessness where there is none. Fake worship conveys an appearance of piety where there is only a desire to be entertained. We settle for fakery whenever the costs and risks entailed by reality are too high and the benefits gained by feigning are too alluring to pass up.

Long-term exposure to fake things makes real things seem overly dull, demanding, expensive, messy, complicated, and pretentious. Those raised on watermelon candy will find actual watermelon not sweet enough. Anyone raised on comic book movies will not find *Hamlet* or *Paradise Lost* sufficiently exciting. Anyone raised on Big Macs will find French onion soup too pungent, or else not sweet enough, not fatty enough, or not salty enough.

In reducing real things to their most obvious and enjoyable qualities, a fake also skims off the diversity and variety found in reality. An honest-to-God head of blond hair contains hundreds of slight gradations and variations of color, but fake blond hair is uniform. A pint of real blueberries will contain a hundred variations of flavor—some more or less tart, some more or less sweet, some green, some vegetal. Fake blueberry skims off all the variety and complexity and reduces the flavor to what is most likable and most easily identifiable. A fake Chanel handbag looks real from twenty feet away and that's all it needs to do, because the purpose of the bag is to convey to others that the owner is rich, which is the same thing a real Chanel handbag accomplishes. But because the cost of the fake is far lower, nothing need be sacrificed to give others this impression.

People prefer what is special, mediocre, and fake to what is holy, natural, and real because the latter categories are largely outside of our control and are usually established according to highly particular rules. The holy is indifferent to our preferences, but the special obeys our whims and conforms to our tastes. In everything traditional and everything which has lasted, modern men will discern both likable and unlikable qualities. Worship, marriage, art, law, justice, architecture . . . any ancient human endeavor which provides stability and identity will invariably contain something which later generations find distasteful, complicated, baroque, silly, inconvenient, difficult, or annoying. Once modern men discern that traditional things offer certain advantages, they are always tempted to say, "There is an awful lot about this I like. But I don't like everything about it. Perhaps I can keep the parts I like and remove the parts that are distasteful and annoying." However, if traditional things work just as well without the distasteful and unlikable parts, some sage would have removed those parts a long time ago. The parts of old things that modern men do not like are exactly what make old things work. We want to divorce childbearing from sex, calories from food, psychic pain from perversity, boredom from intellection, contemplation from worship, the past from the present. We want to banish any and all stress or anxiety from life as a whole, even though all the things we want to banish make a good and productive life possible. Society carries on because traditional things are usually a bit unpleasant and the unpleasant parts are what subject our wills to the limits of nature.

Different Kinds of Fakes

Having acknowledged that fake things are not phantasms, we may inquire about fake movies, fake music, and fake books. A fake movie is not a movie which does not exist, but one which takes no interest in transcendent things and exists merely to provoke the lust of the flesh and the pride of life. If a fake Chanel handbag can truly hold a phone and a wallet, a fake movie can truly excite and amuse. Of course, fake breasts can also excite and amuse, but they cannot sustain an infant's life. The fact that something stirs the soul or inflames the passions is no guarantee that it is real. Uncommon books like the *Odyssey* and *Jane Eyre* are sometimes thrilling, sometimes comic, and sometimes witty, and yet most of the pages are merely observational and contemplative, not qualities which those acclimatized to pleasure find attractive or even comprehensible. Of course, the thrilling, comic, witty passages of a book make it enjoyable, and yet the mediocre impulse is to create books which are nothing but those passages which are easiest to enjoy. It creates music which is nothing but the highs of the "Hallelujah" chorus, romance that is nothing but orgasms, pizza that is nothing but toppings, worship that is nothing but ecstasy, film that is nothing but action, theology that is nothing but politics, and politics that are nothing but protest.

Mediocre things offer an astronomically high exchange rate for those wanting to trade their time for sensual pleasure. The exchange rate offered by common things is much lower, and uncommon things do not deal with human beings according to such economies. The modern world offers mediocre versions of everything from corkscrews to Christianity, and so the man who agrees to the high exchange rate offered by mediocre movies has not simply proven he has lousy taste in film. Rather, he has admitted something to himself about the sort of compromises he is willing to make for pleasure. Film is not the only artistic medium that will ask him to exchange his time for sensual delights: the radio will also make such offers, as will the bookstore, the record store, the grocery store, various political movements, fashionable churches, and social media platforms. Taste in film cannot be sequestered from taste in books, taste in theology, taste in ethics, and so forth. The man who is willing to waste his time on trashy movies is simply a man who is willing to waste his time. He does not become prudent and circumspect simply because he has moved from the theater to the nave of a church. Taste does not act like a discrete object but like a gas which distributes itself equally in the halls of the soul. We know intuitively that the man who is enraptured by the latest blockbuster films and listens to the most popular music is probably not a person who willingly attends a church wherein "traditional worship" is practiced. On the other hand, to learn that someone who loves old books also loves old music and attends Latin mass is not terribly surprising.

It is no wonder, then, that a great number of Christian children raised on mediocre culture summarily abandon the faith once they enter college. The self-professed enemies of God have taught them how to feel.

While the love of God is not exactly like taste in films and books, neither are the two matters wholly unrelated. Scripture consistently presents salvation as a gift appropriate to people who are willing to "receive their good things later," while mediocrity offers pleasure now and trains people to refuse the difficult intellectual work of learning to love beauty. Beauty is sensual and pleasant, but it is not *purely* sensual, thus David Bentley Hart's claim that beauty "seems to promise a reconciliation beyond the contradictions of the moment."[1] Beautiful things are a bonding of the physical and the spiritual; thus the enjoyment of beauty is the unification of sense and intellect. Beauty is a royal treaty between the body and the soul wherein the significant interests of both kingdoms are simultaneously honored. On the other hand, mediocrity is the body's demand that the soul surrender unconditionally. Mediocre things starve the soul, deplete the spiritual soil of nutrients, and train the body to demand good things now—and not just a few good things, but as many good things as the body can physically handle. Mediocre things train people to find the Bible difficult, the Psalms dull, and true prayer ridiculously stuffy.

The Shallows

In the same way that no particular bite of cake makes a man fat and no particular cigarette gives a man lung cancer, no particular pop song makes a man shallow. Not every uncommon thing is holy and not every mediocre thing is "sinful." The use of pornography is sinful, of course, and one could easily argue that pornography has established many outposts beyond what are conventionally known as "dirty magazines" and "dirty movies," for a good deal of what now passes as popular entertainment is replete with pornographic scenes, pornographic lyrics, and joking references to extreme sexual degradation. Secular sympathists love crafting lavish defenses of pornographic pop and stodgy traditionalists never tire of condemning such defenses.

Nonetheless, the danger of mediocrity is not simply one of exposure to explicit sex, for family-friendly films and books are stocked with mindless spectacle and soul-crushing sensuality as often as films and books marketed to libidinous teenagers and maturity-deferring singles. Physical strength may be developed in a gymnasium, but it is taken everywhere. Likewise, laziness may be cultivated on a couch in the basement, but it follows a man wherever he goes. So, too, it is possible for a man to become dangerously shallow without ever watching or listening to anything which is "sinful."

When we describe a certain man as "shallow," we are using metaphorical language to describe his soul. The shallow man's soul is not deep, but what *is* depth of soul? Why this metaphor?

Modern Christians often talk about souls "getting saved," but the idea that a soul could do anything other than get saved frustrates us. Must souls be deep in order to be saved? If shallow people can be saved, what use is there in cultivating a deep soul? Do saved deep souls ultimately receive something from God which He holds back from saved shallow souls? Beneath such questions is the tireless, cowardly fear that what we do with our lives actually matters. Modern Christians do not often talk of shallowness because the word confirms our fears that the human soul may exist in more than just two states: saved and damned. Being shallow is not the same thing as being damned, although a man who thinks himself saved is nonetheless troubled by the accusation that he is shallow. There are spiritual conditions apart from being saved that reasonable people find desirable.

A shallow man lacks spiritual depth because he does not love things which last. Deep love and enduring love are one and the same. The longer a man loves something, the more deeply that thing grows down into his soul. The soul expands to accommodate deep, enduring love. But because shallow things do not last, neither does our love for them, and so the souls of those who love mediocre things are never given a reason to expand. By the time mediocre things are on the verge of laying down roots, we pluck them from our hearts and plant something else instead.

While it is possible to love the same mediocre things for a lifetime, there is rarely incentive to do so. Let us suppose the year is 1989 and an eighth-grade boy sneaks into a showing of *Road House*, then later tells his friends it is "his new favorite movie." What has impressed the boy is not the complex themes of the film but the bloody fistfights, the topless actresses, and Patrick Swayze's nonchalant ability to impose law and order. When the boy reaches college in 1994, though, *Color of Night* is released, which is a far bloodier film with even more nudity, more convincing portrayals of human depravity, and another lead actor who conveys masculinity according to the most current standards. Anyone who has seen *Color of Night* and maintains the opinion that *Road House* is better must appeal to some quality in the film other than spectacle, but this is not possible because both films are shallow and sensational, and so the boy quickly transfers his allegiance from the earlier film to the later.

Of course, in the years following *Color of Night*, a great host of films have been released which feature even more graphic nudity and violence (in keeping with the most current standards), which means that those raised on films like *Road House* have less and less reason to return to them. Such films never have time enough with their audiences to grow, to unfurl through the mind and deepen the soul. If the appeal of a certain blockbuster is that it features so many explosions, so many stunts, so many computer-generated worlds, aliens, guns, jets, and buxom actresses in various states of undress, then even a computer could calculate the story necessary to make the sequel a success. It is rather easy to make a film more sensual than the last—one simply needs more dynamite, guns, aliens, and skin. However, making a more profound sequel requires a deeper soul, not deeper pockets.

Vexing Fidelity

Because spiritual depth is rare, we are willing to return to deep things over and over again. We return not because we like them but because we are lost without them. We return to these things until we become as deep as they are, but we give up on fake things as soon as new ones come along, for the promises of the new things have not yet been revealed as lies. Fake things are easy to love because we only have to love them for a little while and don't need to feel guilt for abandoning them whenever loving them becomes difficult. Old things are hard to love, though, and not just because modernity has villainized the past, but because the things which last are always confrontational, offensive, and unimpressed with our most prized claims of progress.

Like old people, old books rarely tell us what we want to hear. No matter what stage of life a man finds himself in, men in the next stage invariably tell him that he ought to complain less, save more money, drink less, and perhaps simply enjoy life less than he already does. While I am not yet an old man, my students regularly come to me for spiritual counsel. The advice I give is never surprising or exciting. I tell them there's no point to dating in high school. I tell them their parents are more important than their friends, because very few people maintain high school friendships for all that long after high school. I tell them they are neither old enough nor wise enough to lead Bible studies and that as opposed to relying on the Holy Spirit to guide their words, they should pray that the Holy Spirit will give them the humility to be silent. I tell them that if they really want to become competent writers, they will need to give up all their social media accounts. I tell them that as opposed to taking Ritalin, they should try quitting video games for a few months first. I have largely given up celebrating with students who are accepted into prestigious universities because so many of my students lose their faith in God while studying at such places. The longer I teach teenagers, the more I care for them, and the more I care for them, the fewer pleasant pieces of advice I have to offer them. They want me to affirm their impulses, their insights, and the simple paths to happiness they have laid out for themselves. But I cannot in good conscience do so.

Old books are similarly harrowing. Uncommon things last because they bear witness to God and to human nature, neither of which change. They ignore our desire to dismiss what the past teaches about both so that we can create a naïve optimism favorable to our present goals. Uncommon things remind us of our limits, our frailty, and the fact that any cultural project worth undertaking will only reach fulfillment after we have passed from this life to the next. For the modern man, lasting books are a distressing reminder of what our ancestors thought, said, and did in order to create the modicum of stability that we, their enlightened grandchildren, now use as a rallying point from which we may march to their graves and desecrate their corpses. A love of uncommon things produces a deep distrust of the latest promises that poverty, violence, oppression, and bigotry could be cured if we would only liquidate what little remains of tradition and custom. A few gullible conservatives can always be found who think that the latest utopian promises are authentic, and thus those who are faithful to lasting things must regularly endure accusations from friends and foes alike that the whole world could be happy if they would simply give up their absurd obsession with the past.

Because fake things do not last, they discourage us from developing lifelong relationships with works of art that can provide cohesion and unity to our lives. An uncommon piece of music like Fauré's Requiem or Beethoven's Ninth Symphony will sustain seventy years of devotion and investigation. The boy who discovers Beethoven's Ninth at the age of sixteen knows that such music has something to offer him in every stage of life, whether he is sick or healthy, rich or poor. If he lives to see his ninetieth birthday, Beethoven's Ninth will still have the power to enthrall him. On the other hand, the boy who listens to fashionable pop music knows he will not listen to such music when he becomes an old man. He is perhaps even a little disgusted by the thought, and though he cannot explain this disgust, it grows from an innate knowledge that fake things appeal to us on a purely sensual level. Because the bodies of the elderly are no longer capable of sustaining intense sensual pleasure, it disturbs the young to see them desperately try. The old man who tries to delight in music about cheap sex, fast cars, drug use, drunkenness, power, self-love, self-expression, and money is an unsettling memento mori. The elderly will soon be dead, and what can such music possibly mean to them then?

Fake things trap us in the present and rob us of a reason to think about the future because we know intuitively that the future is a place where things are revealed for what they truly are. The future always unmasks, uncovers, and lays bare, but shallow people are incapable of caring about the future. The shallow man is concerned only with appearances, and so he is blown from one agreeable illusion to the next and never lingers long enough on anything to repair, refine, or revere it. He feeds on the gloss, then flees.

Endnotes

1. David Bentley Hart, *The Beauty of the Infinite*, 16.

9.

On Heirlooms

"Good things are easily destroyed, but not easily created."

—*Roger Scruton*

hile progressives have great contempt for the past, they often have a more accurate sense of the past's worth than conservatives do. Naïve and unrefined conservatives are sometimes willing to sell off huge tracts of the past at cut rates, but the progressives who buy it up never underestimate its worth. Because traditional things are so profoundly valuable, progressives are constantly angling for conservatives to give them up. The person who controls icons of the past also has some power over everyone whose identity is represented by those icons.

The Psychic Burden of Traditions

Let us suppose that on her twenty-first birthday, a young woman (whom we shall call Julia) inherits from her mother a quilt

which has been in the family for six generations. Julia and her
mother stand before an open wooden chest in the attic which
contains nothing other than the quilt. Before removing it from
the chest, Julia learns that the quilt was made by her ancestors
when they lived in Pennsylvania, and she is warned that it is
worth a good deal of money. It has not lately acquired this worth
but has slowly accrued it over a long period of time. Julia's mother tells her that the quilt must be stored in a dry location, that
it should only be used in the winter, and that she must find an
appropriate place to store it when she is not using it. Then Julia's
mother removes the quilt from the chest and unfolds it for her
daughter to see. The edges and seams reveal very little wear and
tear. Julia has never thought of her mother as a severe woman,
yet her lessons and instructions on the quilt have been touched
with a curious curtness and the hint of a short temper. Julia's
mother does not tell the young woman that she may not sell
the quilt because such commands are meaningless. The fact is,
Julia is perfectly free to sell the quilt because no coercive power
can physically restrain her from doing so—this is what makes
the quilt so valuable, though Julia has not yet grasped this. She
knows that certain old things are worth a lot of money, like base-
ball cards and first editions of famous books, but she doesn't
know *why* they are worth so much. Julia's mother explains how
their ancestors moved from Pennsylvania to New York after the
Civil War, then from New York to Norfolk around the time of
the Second World War. Her mother tells Julia that her great-un-
cle committed suicide in 1952 and that the family was left nearly
destitute for three years. A number of other family tragedies are
mentioned: alcoholism, cancer, heart attacks, abuse, a car wreck.
Then her mother hands Julia a check for five hundred dollars.

Julia is delighted until she learns that some of this money must be spent on a new chest for the quilt, one which will fit in Julia's small apartment, and that the rest should be used to have the quilt professionally cleaned once every three years. "This afternoon, we will take the quilt to a woman who will clean it for us," says Julia's mother, "and then we will go find some means by which you can safely stow the quilt." Speaking of the quilt seems to draw Julia's mother to a more sophisticated diction and grammar which makes Julia laugh just a little on the inside. Her twenty-first birthday proves painfully dull.

For several years after taking custody of the quilt, Julia more or less forgets about it. It is safely housed in a zippered case inside the closet where she keeps luggage and the ski boots she never uses. She graduates from college, moves into a career at a bank, casually dates several men, and occasionally attends church. Her life unfolds evenly and predictably until the day she attends the state fair with a friend. They walk through several large tented galleries wherein judges are assessing collections of vegetables and photographs and a small coterie of pudgy old men intently sample a wide assortment of cakes and pies. When they arrive at a vast display of quilts and crocheted items which have been entered into competition, her friend comments on the astronomical value of some quilts. Julia asks what sort of price an old one will fetch, and her friend responds, "Some of them are worth thousands of dollars." Julia wonders how much hers is worth.

The following month, Julia loses her job at the bank and contemplates moving back in with her parents. She has no savings and keeps a high balance on her credit cards. Before phoning her mother to ask about her old room, she remembers the quilt, makes a few phone calls, and schedules a meeting with an antiques appraiser. At this point, Julia tells herself that she is more than willing to move back in with her parents and simply wants to see about the quilt's current value. If it is only worth two or three thousand dollars, it would do her little good to sell it because such a small sum could only keep her afloat for another month or so and this convenience would not be worth her mother's eternal disappointment. As she drives to the appraiser, Julia tells herself that if the quilt is worth more than ten thousand dollars, she will need to seriously consider parting with it. But she seriously doubts that it is worth so much.

When the appraiser sees the quilt, he asks Julia if she is considering selling it. Julia tells him she is not sure. He tells her that the quilt is unusual and that he will need a little while to examine it. She leaves, returning later with a cup of coffee, at which point the appraiser begins a lengthy and very technical description of the quilt which is unfamiliar to Julia. He makes a number of comments about the stitching, the thread, the fabric, the design. He even knows the name of the county in Pennsylvania where the quilt was made. He finishes the description with a few awed claims about the rarity of such work and the immaculate condition of the item. He believes that the quilt will fetch somewhere between eighty and ninety thousand dollars at auction and then begins telling her about his commission, the dates of the next auction, and so forth. "How much," Julia interrupts, "would this quilt have brought at an auction twenty-five years ago?" The appraiser tells her he saw a few similar quilts sell for forty thousand dollars when he first became an antiques dealer. "How much would the quilt have fetched fifty years ago?" The appraiser tells Julia it might have sold for ten thousand dollars, then begins a few predictable comments about inflation. Julia tells the appraiser she will need to think the matter over, packs up her quilt, and leaves. As the evening comes, Julia begins to understand why old things are so valuable.

The price of the quilt rises over time because with each passing generation, the act of selling it becomes a more grievous betrayal of a growing number of one's ancestors. At the point Julia receives the heirloom, six mothers have thought it better for their children to receive the quilt than for the value of the quilt to be liquidated in a sale. Compared with the quilt's symbolic value, its functional value is quite small, for it might be auctioned off for a fortune and easily replaced with a used quilt purchased at a secondhand store for a few dollars. For this reason, heirlooms are a psychic burden on those who possess them. They are acquired freely but are expensive to keep because their custodians must voluntarily renounce their economic value. To renounce the economic value of an heirloom is an act of faith that the soul matters more than the body, but this act of faith is also its own reward because it instills greater respect for the family name. In turn, greater respect for the family name leads to a greater desire that the family name not be shamed. Thus heirlooms impose high standards of virtue on their possessors. Heirlooms are not so much representations of a family as they are embodiments of it. If, after seven generations, a certain son finally buckles to greed and converts an heirloom into cash, the family name does not suddenly disappear, but the meaning of the name is obscured because the present generation no longer owns an ancient gift with which to welcome the coming generation into the family. Furthermore, heirlooms are icons which depict the suffering our parents have endured to raise us, for the moment the former generation relinquishes the heirloom to the heir, they have overcome the long and painful temptation to live easily at the expense of their children's existential stability.

If a man thinks highly of his ancestors, he will not betray them for thirty pieces of silver, but neither will he be apt to thoughtlessly begin an affair, become drunk in public, or commit apostasy or blasphemy, all of which reflect poorly on his upbringing and his parents' upbringing. Unless a man respects the people, places, and institutions from which his identity is derived—and respects them more than he respects himself—he has no incentive to live in a worthy manner.

Liquidating the Gospel

At the same time, if the people, places, and institutions which have the power to confer identity do not also have costly heirlooms to pass on to new generations, those who receive the identity will regard it cheaply. They will not fear bringing shame upon it.

In the last century, American churches have become more and more like nightclubs, burlesques, and movie theaters because rationalists have told Christians that going to church is a foolish waste of time. Christians themselves have generally come to believe that this is true, and thus Christians have come to believe that any church would be lucky to have their attendance. Accordingly, Christians no longer think of making themselves worthy of church membership—rather, they expect churches to make themselves worthy of members. Churches are filled with people who think more highly of themselves than their denominations, which naturally degrades the glory of the denomination and makes future generations uninterested in the identity their churches offer. If everyone in the congregation values his own opinions over the dogmas of his church, he will be little interested in bestowing a lasting gift on his church which will lead subsequent generations to respect the identity which the church offers, and so every generation remakes worship in their own image.

American Christians cannot talk about loyalty for more than two seconds without severely hedging their bets and stating their limits and caveats. When one Christian tells another where he goes to church, he often immediately begins stating all the things about his church that he does not approve of, like the music or the sermons or the theology. We are willing to accept the identity our churches offer so long as they do not discomfort or embarrass us. We invent bizarre, hypothetical circumstances in which we would part with our churches, and then use these unlikely scenarios to gain leverage over our churches in the present. We think it is reasonable to always be skeptical simply because we can imagine the man at the pulpit telling us to do awful things.

Liquidating the Canon

What is true of heirlooms is true of uncommon things, as well, for classic books and music and works of art constitute a cultural inheritance which similarly places a profound psychic burden on those who receive it. Classic works of art are to culture what heirlooms are to families. For thousands of years, Homer, Plato, Aristotle, and Virgil have become glorious as one generation after another has illuminated their works not only through private devotion, but also through public adoration of their wisdom.

Homer occupies a massive estate within the canon because his work has been handed down for more than one hundred generations. If the value of a fine quilt increases so dramatically over the course of six generations, what is a book like the *Iliad* worth? While the *Iliad* is not the private possession of a single family, like a quilt or an old clock or a strand of pearls, it is nonetheless an inheritance which has survived an arduous trek through the centuries to arrive in the present day. Each generation which has received Homer has thought it better to read the *Iliad* and the *Odyssey* than to commit the same intellectual and spiritual energies to some lately published book which flatters the reader. It is not enough to simply keep the *Iliad* and the *Odyssey* in print for anyone who happens to want them, because classic works are only preserved from one generation to the next by way of public adoration. The younger generation will only read Homer if they have seen the older generation do so; any man who wants his grandchildren to read Homer must read Homer himself. Simply passing down a case of cheap paperback editions will not do because access to classics is not enough. Every American has access to Homer and almost nobody reads him. Homer is taught in schools because schools are the only place where people can be forced to read Homer, and keeping Homer alive requires as much force as we can muster. Outside of schools, most of the people who read Homer are forcing themselves to do so.

Nevertheless, in the same way that the value of an antique quilt can be liquidated, so can the profound value of Homer and Plato and the like. If the dozen or so greatest authors in the canon were forcibly expelled from their thrones, the palace might be razed and thousands of cheap apartments constructed from the ruins. If universities remove just Homer and Shakespeare, the amount of space which would open up in their absence could comfortably accommodate fifty contemporary authors. Similarly, the young woman who sells an antique quilt can purchase a new car, a two-month-long vacation to Paris, and a complete wardrobe from Chanel with the profits. She might even donate a thousand dollars to charity to salve her conscience.

The modern impulse is always to calculate the liquidated value of precious old things like Judas calculating the worth of the woman's jar of oil. Once liquidated, the value could be redistributed among a greater number of people. Thus, anything glorious—anything splendid, deeply rooted, beautiful, and imbued with transcendent meaning—is necessarily selfish, for it keeps its value to itself. In the French Revolution, the accumulated wealth of kings, aristocrats, and clergy was seized and put to a more equitable use. In the American Revolution, the accumulated power of the king was seized and broadly dispersed among the people. Democracy simply does with power what socialism does with capital, for both are fundamentally concerned with liquidation and redistribution. "Power corrupts and absolute power corrupts absolutely," argues the Republican, who believes that no one man should inherit more power than another. "Yes," replies the Marxist, who believes that no man should inherit more wealth than another. "Money corrupts, as well, and great sums of money corrupt all the more." For every objection the Republican has to the socialist's conception of wealth, the monarchist has a similar objection to the Republican's conception of power.

While money can be evenly redistributed, purchasing power cannot, for one man can do more with a million dollars than a million men can do with a dollar each. The same is true of power and glory, which only exist in contrast to their lack. To have any power is to have more than another does, for two equal powers set against one another are stagnant. Likewise, glory exists only in comparative accumulations. The top of a pyramid is the most glorious part, but the glory of the pyramid's peak cannot be redistributed among each stone in the edifice without leveling it. The redistribution of glory is indistinguishable from the immolation of glory.

Once the value of an heirloom has been liquidated, it quickly disappears. Quilts made in nineteenth-century New England are valuable because they are securely bound by honor to the families that have possessed them for generations. The price offered for an old quilt must be high enough to overwhelm the custodian's sense of duty. However, once a quilt exits the family that created it, the new owner must be careful not to turn around and resell it too quickly because the value of an heirloom is based on its perceived spiritual worth. The courtship which leads a woman to take her first or second lover is far more costly than the courtship which leads to her fiftieth lover.

Converting a thing's spiritual value into economic value, as one does when selling an heirloom, is commonly known as "a Faustian bargain." The devil is always willing to trade physical goods for spiritual ones. Money has no spiritual value, which is why the love of money is the root of spiritual corruption. When universities scrub their humanities programs of classic texts, they invariably replace them with contemporary texts that have "the power to change things"—but once the seal of tradition has been broken, things can be changed endlessly. As someone who has been involved in private education for many years, I can tell you that no subject taught at Christian schools undergoes more revisions from year to year than theology, but this is because few Christian schools are willing to host a senior theology class that involves a patient, year-long reading of St. Augustine's *City of God*. Parents want their children to be prepared to "change the world," so they demand that their children read fashionable theological books about wellness, gender, race, social reform, apologetics, creationism, and other hot-button topics. The Christian school which finally liquidates a twenty-year history of teaching the *City of God* will quickly tire of whatever books replace it. No one needs a teacher to explain pop theology books, and thus class seems a waste of time. If a new book is difficult to understand, students do not believe the struggle to be worthwhile, for once they have discerned the book's meaning, the ideas contained in it will no longer be fashionable. Students are quick to intuit that any book which arrives suddenly can depart just as suddenly as well.

This is not an argument against the writing of new books or music, but it is an argument against schools, universities, and churches exchanging the glory of old things for the ease and power of new ones. It is true that anyone who defends old things along these lines is bound to encounter a naysayer who points out that the works of Homer, Bach, and Shakespeare have not always been old, and that when the *Goldberg Variations* debuted, it was not regarded as anything other than pop music. However, the glory of Bach depends not only on the transcendent beauty of his music but also on the costly preservation of this beauty over time. Every heirloom was once a common household item, but the fact that it was once common proves nothing. Most uncommon things come from common origins just as most holy things come from secular origins. The test of time not only proves the spiritual mettle of a thing, it also creates that mettle.

Whereas most things which are fathered by time are then vampirically devoured a little while later, uncommon things have a synergistic relationship with time. Time gives uncommon things meaning, and uncommon things return meaning to time. Anyone who claims that a certain heirloom is "just a quilt" or "just a clock" is incapable of looking beyond appearances. Those who dismiss the *Goldberg Variations* as "the pop music of Bach's day" do so to justify the shallow, appearance-driven musical styles of their own day.

Taming and Devouring

Time tears bodies apart, but souls are immune to the ravages of time. Uncommon artists are capable of investing their souls so deeply into their work that the substances which receive their souls—the stone, paint, paper, canvas, wood, and word—take on spiritual properties. There is a way to love the immaterial God through material means such that the materials do not break under the heavy-leaning weight of time. Instead, as time pours into them, they grow. Time is powerful and terrible, but love can tame time. When you taste a fine Pecorino, you are not merely tasting milk, but milk and time. The Acropolis is stone which has tamed time. The blue in the windows of the Chartres Cathedral is a color which has tamed time. Wine is grape juice which has tamed time. The Nicene Creed is a poem which has tamed time.

We tire of mediocre things because they are soulless, which leaves them with no means of resisting the ravages of time and thus they quickly fall apart. A wildly popular song is like a fresh zebra carcass on the African veldt. In the beginning, a surge of interest draws a great number of beasts to come and feed, but over the coming days the corpse is slowly picked apart and every time a vulture returns to eat, his meal is a little smaller. Likewise, in the months immediately following the release of some ultra-pleasant, mediocre song, it might play once an hour on the radio to satisfy popular demand, but eventually listeners reach the point where they have "heard the song too often" and turn against it. Every purely sensual work of art is condemned to the same quick path to obsolescence.

If a song or film or food has no spiritual or intellectual value, it does not matter how pleasant the thing is because pleasure in itself cannot satisfy. Pleasure takes place in the body, but satisfaction takes place in the soul. Great art is satisfying because it creates bonds between body and soul, but mediocre art uses exaggerated offers of pleasure to seduce the body away from the soul in much the same way that an antiques dealer must offer an intellectually overwhelming sum for a priceless family heirloom. Our bodies are hungry and our souls are hungry, but we are tempted to starve the soul in order to stuff the body because it is more pleasant now. Returning over and over again to a song which is merely pleasant (one which merely feeds the body) eventually reveals that the song is meaningless. Words only have meaning in the context of other words, and music only has meaning within the context of human experience. Returning too often, too quickly to a certain word or song divorces it from the world which gives it meaning. If a man listens to a certain song too many times in a row, he will cease to hear it, just as repeating a word over and over turns it into phonetic gibberish.

A Pornographic Culture

Because uncommon things are not purely sensual, we do not feel the need to return to them over and over again ad nauseam. Uncommon things often have the calendar on their side as well, for many are tied to holidays, which slows down our exposure to them. But mediocre things have no relationship with time, which is why they are often consumed at night, in secret, in rapid succession. The relatively mild pornography of the 1950s and 1960s was both sold and consumed in highly limited, self-contained magazines and movie tickets. The more accessible and extreme pornography has become, the less it satisfies. The man who took home a copy of *Playboy* in 1953 was limited to the dozen or so photographs contained between the covers; however, the modern man has access to unlimited quantities of pornography and may peruse many thousands of images every time he gives in to lust. The more quickly he burns through these images, however, the more vexing he finds the human body, for he proves with every click and every screen he scrolls through that the human body cannot satisfy him. This is why pornography has become increasingly vile in the internet age. We are bored and frustrated with human beings whom we encounter as soulless bodies because they cannot say meaningful things, teach us, converse with us. That boredom and frustration is now cathartically loosed not merely through performances of sexual exploitation and degradation, but violence.

10.

Social Media and Child-rearing

"People who cannot bear to be alone are generally the worst company."
—*Albert Guinon*

Without question, the most plentiful supply of mediocrity in the world today comes not from radio stations or movie theaters or streaming services but from social media. Over the last several years, we have found ourselves lying awake in bed for hours every night, looking at our phones, hastily scrolling through posts from friends which we have already seen, desperate for something new, and even more bored than we were when we checked earlier in the day. Unlike an addiction to drugs, alcohol, or nicotine, our addiction to social media offers no momentary pleasure and no escape from the pressures of the day. Facebook, Twitter, and Instagram *are* the pressures of the day, and yet we return to them again and again, hoping that something new, euphoric, or mildly satisfying will appear so that we can be done with our searching. What kind of man does something every day, over and over again, from which he derives no pleasure, no enjoyment, and no profit? A slave. A captive.

A number of clinical studies have been conducted which examine the effects of social media on the brain, and the results are quite grim. However, one need not be a social scientist or medical doctor to note how regular use of social media makes people depressed, agitated, and more easily bored.

Recreational use of cell phones has replaced smoking as the go-to bad habit of people who are just standing around, but convincing people to put away their cell phones and delete their social media accounts has proven far more difficult than convincing people to quit smoking. While social media will not give a man heart disease, which is a medically diagnosable condition, it will make him shallow; however, unlike heart disease, shallowness is a condition that afflicts a part of man for which he is unconcerned: the soul.

I have argued that the essence of mediocrity is ephemerality, and social media is nothing if not ephemeral. Whether a picture, a video, or a passing thought on the state of the world, the average post on social media is encountered, assessed, enjoyed, and abandoned in a matter of seconds, then forgotten forever. As such, social media highly incentivizes cleverness, sexiness, shock, and spectacle, the four cornerstones of mediocrity. A meme is only funny once or twice. Instagram is chock-full of interchangeable pictures of nearly identical models posting nearly the same pictures of themselves every day. Facebook and Twitter are well-stocked repositories of outlandish political claims which are quickly conceived, quickly read, and quickly forgotten. Almost nothing on social media is worth a second look.

In the course of authoring this book, I deleted my Facebook,

Instagram, and Twitter accounts, all of which had occupied hours of my life on a daily basis for more than a decade. After eleven years of increasingly heavy use, I could not take seriously my own excuses for remaining on social media. Toward the end, I found that I no longer paused to mull over anything I saw on Facebook, and yet the more bored I became, the more time I gave over to it. When considering this pathetic truth, I also recalled standing before El Greco's *Christ Carrying the Cross* for the first time at the Metropolitan Museum of Art, after which I sat down on a nearby bench and gazed at the painting for more than half an hour. Benches are set up in every other room of a decent museum for just such a purpose. The curators and creators of a museum assume that the paintings are baffling and overwhelming, and yet they are also confident that with time, they can be understood more clearly and penetrate more deeply into the soul. By contrast, I knew that most of what I posted on Facebook wasn't worth reading once, let alone twice. Most of it was unimportant, reactionary, timely, amusing at best—in other words, a complete waste of my time and the time of anyone who read it.

During the decade in which I maintained my social media accounts, I found myself increasingly willing to look at Facebook and Instagram during the in-between moments of my days, by which I mean those two- and three-minute waits which proliferate in a convenience-oriented society. My time on Facebook was not concentrated in a single two-hour passage of the evening. Rather, I checked Facebook while waiting for my eggs to cook, while waiting for the water in the shower to heat up, while waiting for my students to file into class, while waiting in line at the grocery store, the restroom, the doctor's office. I checked Instagram while pumping my gas, while waiting at red lights, while waiting for my dinner to arrive at a restaurant. In a previous life, I had used such moments to consider the day, mull over things I had lately heard, give thanks to God for the lives of my daughters, and speak with my own soul about what it needed.

As a child, I was not much for books. I owe the fact that I grew up to become a teacher of old books and an author to the fact that I did not sleep well when I was young. From an early age, I would lie awake in bed for two or three hours every night, gazing at the ceiling. During the day, I watched entirely too much television and read very little, but at night, I had nothing to do but think. What little strength of my mind I had was preserved by the sleepless hours during which the banality of the day was purged away.

As an adult, I once again found sleep elusive, but now these sleepless hours in bed were frittered away scrolling through an endless sequence of screens, each less satisfying than the one before. In the weeks prior to deleting my Facebook account, I realized that those hours in bed would be better spent doing nothing at all. When Cicero said that man was "Never less alone than when wholly alone, never less idle than when wholly idle," he meant that the human soul is not a mirror image of the body but a companion to the self. While a man is his soul, the soul is also a genuine other. For this reason, a man may talk to himself, reason with himself, and "come to himself" as the prodigal son did in the pigsty of a far-off country. Were a man to betray his principles, he would "not be able to live with himself," which is to say that his soul would chide and trouble him.

Usually, though, the human soul speaks in a "still small voice," one so small that a man will find it drowned out in the company of others (whether at a frat party or a Bible study). On rare occasions, a word or work of art or encounter with the divine may cut through the noise and distraction that surrounds a man and communicate directly to his soul, such as when the Israelites heard St. Peter's Pentecost sermon and were "cut to the heart," as St. Luke writes. However, most of the time, the human soul is a neglected and geriatric father. Every man acts as the son of his own soul and rarely comes to visit and ask what the old man would like to talk about. The soul wants to discuss dull and unflattering matters, like going to church, reading old books, the deleterious effects of pornography, and the importance of sitting quietly, none of which are subjects a man finds very exciting. Uncommon things strengthen the soul because they offer an occasion for the old man to slowly, painfully express his thoughts about God, women, love, art, virtue, piety, truth, and holiness to his young son. The soul has little to say about mediocre things like billion-dollar comic book films, fried tacos, roller coasters, or pop music, however. The soul is no more interested in hearing about such matters than an eighty-four-year-old man would be.

Were you to take a man in his ninth decade of life to see a summer blockbuster on IMAX, he would likely spend the whole time complaining that the film was too loud, too fast-paced, too stupid, and that all the lady superheroes looked like hussies in their latex rompers. But these complaints are no different from the complaints every man's soul makes over such films, even the soul of a young man. A young man simply has a greater ability to drown out the complaints of his soul. To be "wholly alone" and "wholly idle," though, is like being stuck with an old man on a very long car trip without a radio. Under the normal conditions of life, the old man can easily be forgotten, sidestepped, and many excuses invented for not visiting him. But when you're stuck in the car together, one is left with no other option than to speak with the soul. As predictable a story as it is, most people discover in so doing that the old man is actually far better company than the friends with whom they regularly flirt, gossip, and banter.

However, the widespread use of social media has largely eliminated waiting and uncommitted time from our lives, which used to be the occasions upon which we were forced to spend a few minutes alone with our souls. Anyone with a phone need never wait for anything again. We not only consult social media while standing in store lines or sitting in waiting rooms, but during awkward silences, when a film is paused so someone can use the bathroom, while waiting for a church service to begin (or end), during commercials, while driving to work, and a thousand other little respites which were formerly filled with consideration and contemplation. Contemplation is a plant which grows from the soil of boredom. Without the boredom that typically results from a constant and prolonged exposure to sameness, contemplation is not possible.

The Virtue of Dull Films

The average American is a bit bored by old movies and foreign films because of the length of the shots, by which I mean the time that elapses between camera cuts. In the typical contemporary blockbuster film, most shots are between three and five seconds long. On the other hand, many older filmmakers (say, from the 1940s and 1950s) and European filmmakers (those stuffy fellows whose work is reissued by the Criterion Collection) employ shots which last thirty to forty seconds. A subtle but perceptible anxiety develops in modern viewers who are asked to consider a single image or idea for this long, mainly because they know more ideas and images are forthcoming but have not yet arrived.

If a film opens with a shot of an empty living room, how long can the director ask the audience to gaze at that living room before they become bored or even angry? If the audience is only shown the empty living room for two seconds before the director proceeds to the next image (a vase of flowers, a man pushing a child on a swing), all the audience learns is, "This is an empty living room," since very few of the objects that fill the living room can be noted in just two seconds. If the empty living room is shown for ten seconds, however, the audience begins to get frustrated at the pace of the movie. They accuse the director or editor in their hearts, saying, "Yes, yes, a living room. I don't need ten seconds to determine that a living room is a living room." There is a burst of fresh interest with every cut, but the interest only lasts a moment and is based entirely on novelty, which generates a quick but short-lived unsettling of the mind. After three or four seconds of viewing a living room, a sense of sameness settles in and the mind grows restless.

If a director wants his audience to contemplate a living room, he must show it to them long enough that they become bored. If the same shot of a living room is shown for twenty seconds, the audience undergoes a fascinating trajectory. In the first several seconds, they are interested simply because it is new. Then, because the newness is all that yet interests them, their interest quickly declines and they become bored by sameness. Having reached the point of boredom, what happens next depends on the mental strength of each audience member. For some, bore-

dom becomes anger. Others attempt to escape boredom by finding something interesting about the living room, or even making
up something interesting about it. Upon further inspection, this
is not just any living room. Ashtrays, photographs, a musket
hanging on the wall, and a long line of urns on the mantelpiece
make it a very particular living room, though none of these details would have been noticed if the cut occurred before boredom ensued.

Films with long shots ask more of the audience than a film
with many cuts. If a film opens with a full minute of an empty
living room, the director is telling the audience, "If you're going
to enjoy this film, you have to be the kind of person who can
find an empty living room interesting." The longer the director
holds a single shot (especially a shot in which there is no movement), the more insistent he is that there *is* something interesting, something more to notice. Shallow people find such movies
aggravating because they assume there is nothing beyond mere
appearances, but this is because they have remade the world in
their own image.

By contrast to a dull film, an action film moves faster than
the speed of boredom. This makes it akin to social media, as
the speed at which a man devours a feed is up to him and he is
not required to pause on anything, to dwell on anything. Shortly
before I deleted my Instagram account, I found myself scrolling
through images at a speed which outpaced my boredom—as opposed to moving on from an image when I got bored, I moved
on before I got bored. By spreading my consumption diffusely
throughout the day, I managed to avoid moments when I had to
think my way out of boredom, distracting myself instead with
things that I would never again return to.

Justifications

A great many people justify the use of social media on the grounds that it increases the size of their community, which they claim enlarges the soul. "Community" has become our most cherished virtue.

Community is an old word and an old concept, but in ages past, one always spoke of a particular community: the Seattle community, the monastic community, the queer community. A community was seen as a thing every bit as objective as a lamp, a table, a pen, or a vase. However, during the last twenty years, community has been transformed from a concrete object into a spiritual abstraction. School and church websites *could* claim, "Our community is very important to us," but they more often say, "Community is very important to us." This refusal to identify which community is important grants community a universal status and value.

"Building community" has become the goal of high school basketball programs, neighborhood barbecues, public service projects, family game nights, staff Christmas parties, and summer workshops. Not only has "community" been transformed from a thing into an abstraction, but we also demand no further justification for things which "foster" or "build community," for we regard all instances of community as inherently good. We care relatively little about what the community does, provided it "brings us closer together." As such, we genuinely believe that amusing and entertaining ourselves together is important and good.

Christians are hardly alone in their obsession with "community." Nearly every corporate website in existence (from Pfizer to Philip Morris) proudly proclaims that it is both a community unto itself and a boon to whatever preexistent community it finds itself in. They all invest in their communities, serve their communities, give back to their communities, make a difference in their communities, support their communities. Such claims are never buried in the corners of company websites but are front and center. Were you to go backstage at a local strip club, the manager would probably proudly tell you, "The girls who work here have a really deep sense of community. They all support one another and look after one another."

Despite its omnipresence, purveyors of community speak as though it were a hard thing to come by. "It's hard to find a strong church community anymore," claim thousands of church websites. "It is rare to find a company that cares about building lasting ties with the community," most companies would have us believe. Community is so exceedingly rare, we are told, that wherever a man finds it, he should take what he can get.

Thus, social media has transformed community into a commodity which eucharistically confers virtue on the one who possesses it. But because so much of the community we share is vapid and banal, the rise of community-as-virtue has had a deleterious effect on our taste and on our ability to enjoy good art. We easily excuse the banality of social media because it "brings us together." Nonetheless, there is a profound difference between posting a picture of your dinner for your friends and actually going out to dinner with friends. Going out to dinner with friends is expensive, takes hours, requires preparation, and thus an evening spent at a restaurant is memorable, significant, a way of marking time. What is more, once a group of friends has committed to dinner together, the conversation at the table must be endured and enjoyed as long as the meal goes on. The dull thoughts of one diner cannot be painlessly glossed over but must be suffered or redeemed by everyone else at the table. If other guests are not immediately interesting, we have incentive to figure out ways of making them interesting to ourselves. We can pay closer attention to their stories, ask prying questions which call forth stories which are more compelling, study the subtle changes in their eyes and mouths when they speak of this or that subject. In fact, any solitary and prolonged period of sitting and waiting stands to elongate and expand the imagination—a healthy mind learns to move from boredom to contemplation, while a weak mind passes from boredom to anger.

Dinner with friends might seem a trivial example of the casualties wrought by social media-induced boredom, and yet it is emblematic of the common man's boredom with human beings. Despite the claim that it created community, I found that my years of exposure to social media produced an increasing disinterest or dislike of other people. I found myself less inclined to go out for the evening, less interested in invitations to dinner, less interested in films. Having lost the incentive to make other people interesting to myself, I became more short-tempered. My frustration at being slighted by someone online was far more extreme than being slighted by someone physically present.

In this way, the effects of social media use are not all that different from the effects of looking at pornography. Both lead us to reduce other people to their most interesting and arresting traits, while discounting (or discarding) anyone who does not immediately attract us or grab our attention. The nearly infinite pornographic options now offered to the modern man mean that pornography users have little incentive to find a beautiful woman all that interesting, even a beautiful woman who is completely nude. In a bygone era, a provocatively dressed woman might "stop traffic." However, by the time he is twenty-five, the modern man has already seen so many beautiful nude women—and has access to many millions more—that he can afford to be profoundly picky. Almost nothing satisfies him. Similarly, social media can now put us in touch with people who believe exactly what we believe, whose tastes are interchangeable with our own, and so we have lost patience with everyone who thinks differently than we do. For this reason, social media "conversations" quickly degenerate into vitriolic insults and threats.

New York

Teachers have a unique vantage point from which to observe the changes social media has wrought on the imagination. Eleven years ago, I chaperoned a small class of seniors to New York City for the first time. We attended the Metropolitan, the Frick, and the Cloisters. None of the eighteen students had smartphones, which were not yet an omnipresent feature of American life. The students were free to go where they liked in the museums, but many meandered with me from one painting to the next, and I pointed out various details they were likely to miss. For years, I have regarded that first trip to New York City as an idyll, an unusual and transformative five days in which I figured out a good deal about what it meant to be a teacher. I am yet in regular contact with several students from that trip, whom I now count as friends.

Since this first trip to New York, I have led nine other classes to the Metropolitan and the Cloisters and none of those expeditions have gone as well. With each passing year, students learn and enjoy less and less from the trip. They have ceased to wonder at the great art which we have traveled hundreds of miles to contemplate; instead, they spend their time standing in front of the great art while their friends take pictures of them. On my eighth trip to New York, I was tagged in a shared photo account of all the pictures students had taken on the trip. Two dozen students had taken nearly ten thousand photos in just four days, almost all of which were pictures of themselves blocking a clear view of something beautiful in the background.

When we returned home, I gave the class a questionnaire in which I asked about their favorite parts of the trip, what they had learned, and how they wished it had gone differently. In response to the question, "What do you hope you remember about the trip to New York ten years from now?" all but two students said they would remember growing closer with their classmates and having a good time with their friends. Very few of them mentioned witnessing the timeless art and sculpture, which had been the purpose of the trip.

In their defense, Aristotle comments in his treatise on rhetoric that young people are "fonder of their friends, intimates, and companions than older men are, because they like spending their days in the company of others and have not yet come to value either their friends or anything else by their usefulness to themselves."[1] Their greater interest in friends than beauty is emblematic of their immaturity. At the same time, prior to the age of smartphones and social media, I witnessed students bonding with their friends in New York while gazing at the works of Rembrandt, El Greco, Delacroix, and Mary Cassatt. Beauty was a common interest, and so they talked together, laughed together, and questioned one another about a worthy and ennobling subject. At least, this is how I remembered it.

Thinking that I may have idealized the first trip (or even the second and third, during which few students had smartphones linked to social media accounts), I decided to contact as many old students as possible and to ask them what they recalled from their trip to New York seven or eight years earlier. Most of them said they remembered the beauty of the art at the Metropolitan, the Frick, and the Cloisters. They also remembered the splendor, squalor, and incomprehensible size of the city itself. Since I had seen these students last, they had gone on to college, graduated, and spent time traveling in Europe. They had married and begun having children. When describing for me what they recalled of their trip to New York, few mentioned their friends.

This may be due, in part, to the fact that high school students have many friends but adults do not. When I was in high school, I thought myself deeply and admirably attached to my friends; however, twenty years after graduating, I only speak regularly with one high school friend. These conversations occur once a year, not more often. Of the dozens of friends I made during college, I only speak with one on a regular basis, and I suspect the same is true for most people. We make friends easily in high school because we live near one another, suffer the same indignities at the hands of teachers, participate in the same pastimes, and are all essentially broke and powerless. But when we grow up, we move away and our lives become very distinct. Our old friends come to accept new creeds and many of our high school pastimes begin to strike us as tawdry. What were we doing with our friends that was so important? Very little. Many of our friends were simply accomplices. As adults, the people we work with slowly begin making sense to us, and yet we do not form deep bonds with them because we no longer have as much free time on our hands. When we are not at work, we prefer to be with our families.

In recent years, I have begun explaining this to the class before leaving for New York. I tell them:

> *Strange as it may seem, ten years from now, there is a good chance you will not be in regular contact with any of your high school friends. After high school you will move away, make different friends, and those friends will become more important to you because they live near you, they help you, give you gifts, share your spiritual burdens, tell you to go to church and to not drink so much. Your high school friends won't do that because they'll be far away.*
>
> *I tell you this because when we go to New York, you will be tempted to try to have as good a time as possible with your friends. You will be tempted to talk when you should be silent and laugh when you should be circumspect. Nonetheless, I want your time in New York to be valuable to you for the rest of your lives, which means I am asking you to have a higher goal than a good time. The modern fixation on having a good time means our lives are less and less memorable because we know in our hearts that having fun is really not that important. The love of God is important, the pursuit of virtue is important, the redemption of suffering is important, but the only people who talk about having a good time more than Christians are frat boys and contestants on competitive*

dating programs.

If your primary goal in New York is having a good time with your friends, you won't get a very high return on your time because ten years from now, very few (if any) of your friends will play a significant role in your life. I am not suggesting you should abandon all your high school friends now simply because they won't be involved in your life as an adult, but I am telling you to play the long game. You need to consider what you will have to offer the friends you make ten years from now. If you commit yourself to confronting, contemplating, and appreciating the many works of staggering beauty at the Metropolitan, you can pass your love and understanding of beauty on to the friends you make in the future. Surrendering to beauty now will repay dividends in the future from which other people can profit. You are not morally obligated to have a good time, but you are morally obligated to enrich your soul so you can be glorious mothers and fathers to your children. Do not forsake the more important things for lesser things. The love of a good time makes tourists of us all, but the search for something good and holy is the preoccupation of pilgrims, which is what you all must become.

Thus far, I have not found any class to be baffled upon hearing this. It not only makes sense to them, it explains many of the questions (and suspicions) they have secretly harbored about their parents for years, like why their parents seem to have so few friends and why their parents have such a different idea of what constitutes having "a good time" with their friends.

Special Pleading

The excuses parents offer for their children's use of social media are a microcosm of the ways that all Christians avoid St. Paul's command to "be careful how you live . . . making the best use of your time" (Eph. 5:15–16). Parents have read countless news stories about the dangers of social media; however, the cautions and warnings delivered by school administrators have largely fallen on deaf ears thus far. Despite the fact that science, common sense, and a bevy of expert witnesses have testified to the fact that social media is incredibly addictive and leads to feelings of loneliness, inadequacy, desperation, depression, and anxiety, let alone short attention spans, many parents feel that *their* children are not susceptible to these nasty side effects.

The average Christian mother or father usually argues that their child is different from other kids. He gets good grades. He plays guitar in a worship band, leads a Bible study (or attends one), and takes part in an accountability group. He is fiercely loyal to his friends, is capable of thinking deeply, and participates in meaningful conversations with his parents. He has regular face-to-face meetings with his soccer team and his friends from church, so he is not always stuck behind a screen. In the end, social media might not be great for children, but between school and sports and church, the ill effects of Instagram are more than counterbalanced.

Many parents use good grades to justify their own child-rearing practices, especially the amount of autonomy and discretion they leave up to their teenage sons and daughters. But in America, nearly everyone gets good grades. The same parents who claim that good grades are a sign of spiritual striving are also likely to bully and politic teachers into giving higher scores on occasions when their children get low ones. In and of themselves, good grades prove absolutely nothing. I regularly give good grades to students who seem to be on the road to lives of misery and discontentment, even while they may prove "successful" in a purely material sense of the word. When measuring the goodness of a child's upbringing, both in his life at home and his life at school, grades matter much less than loves. Who are some of your son's favorite poets and sculptors? What Baroque paintings has he put reproductions of in his locker? What songs bring him to tears? What has he learned from the book of Ecclesiastes which will help him choose a good wife? Who was the first philosopher he truly understood? While such questions offer far more accurate assessments of a child's intellect, one may easily imagine them baffling the parent of a student with a perfect grade point average.

Christ teaches, "The student is not above the teacher, but everyone who is fully trained will be like their teacher" (Luke 6:40 NIV). Modern Christians are skeptical of this proverb because their teenage children are nothing like their math teachers, literature teachers, Sunday school teachers, pastors, and priests, but this is because someone is not "a teacher" simply because he stands at the front of a classroom and talks about geometry or Steinbeck.

Parents can determine who their children's teachers are by assessing who their children are trying to become. Who do they dress like? Who do they talk like? Whose opinions on politics and religion do they imitate? Whose preferences do they reproduce when shopping, when choosing a film to watch, or when talking of God?

If a child dresses like a pop musician, talks like a rapper, and cannot turn his gaze away from successful athletes, these are the child's actual teachers. They have shaped and molded his heart. Plenty of students regard the fellow who wears a tie and conjugates verbs from behind a lectern as an obstacle to their real teachers, whose classes they return to every day at three in the afternoon.

While a sixteen- or seventeen-year-old boy is not "fully trained" as Christ's proverb describes, neither can a Christian child become fully "like their teacher" while living at home. After all, Christian parents generally place a number of checks against their sons and daughters embracing the nihilistic lifestyles of the soulless celebrities they lust after. This more often takes place in college, when they are out of the home and can embrace these teachings more fully. The worldview analyst within every father's heart tempts him to say that his son "takes what is good" from the soulless celebrities and entertainers he adores and leaves behind what is bad, but very few human beings can hold out forever against the shallowness and evil they daily seek out.

Handling Evil

In the same way that naïve parents believe their children can "handle" social media by balancing out the shallowness with profundity, I often hear parents talk about the ability of their teenage sons and daughters to "handle" a movie. (Much less frequently, they speak of a teenager's ability to "handle this music" or "handle this book.") The ability to handle a movie is typically staked in the intellectual and spiritual maturity of the handler. A student with greater spiritual maturity is better able to "deal

with" a movie which liberally trades in the obscene, the blasphemous, or the seductive. But what exactly does it mean to handle
a movie? What does it mean to deal with the vulgarity in a film?

The logic runs something like this: Tarantino is a master filmmaker and a rank moralist, but a very mature intellect will be able
to glean what is good from Tarantino while dismissing what is
seductive or vicious or vulgar. The mature intellect is like a sieve,
and everything submitted to this sieve which is not good, true,
or beautiful simply passes through and is not retained. Who is
more vicious, after all: Quentin Tarantino or the Egyptians who
enslaved the people of God? And yet, didn't God require His
people to glean what was valuable from the Egyptians even while
departing from that wicked nation, their gods, and their false
beliefs? Can Christians not do something similar with film and
art and literature?

It is pretty to think the matter is so simple. I don't suppose
that any student raised to evaluate all things from a Christian
worldview—keeping the Christian parts of the world and condemning the non-Christian parts—could be blamed for wanting to test their skills against someone or something truly cunning. But the more crafty the unbelieving filmmaker, the more
challenging the task of identifying the Gnostic and nihilistic
philosophy.

Sometimes Christian parents realize that a little help is needed in the plundering, and so they quiz their children on the philosophical implications of a film while the credits roll. Son, did
you see how the director was glorifying sensuality in that scene?
The light hits the bottle so that the liquor inside is luminous, but
the hero is only reveling in his freedom. He is not using his freedom selflessly. God gives us good things, but we must use them

in the service of others. Parents often expect that these kinds of comments will effectively nullify any deleterious effect that atheist, materialist images and sounds might have made upon their children's minds. Such pious observations put a little weight behind that push to get the objectionable content through the intellect-sieve so that none of those alluring presentations of vice remain.

It is not my contention to contend that a film or book or piece of music must be wholly in keeping with Christian tradition in order to be of value. In St. Gregory of Nyssa's *Life of Moses*, the late antique theologian describes how pagan philosophy must be circumcised by Christian dogma: "For example, pagan philosophy says that the soul is immortal. There is a pious offspring. But it also says that souls pass from bodies to bodies and are changed from a rational to an irrational nature. This is a fleshly and alien foreskin. . . . And one could describe in some detail how good doctrines are contaminated by profane philosophy's absurd additions. When these are completely removed, the angel of God comes to us in mercy, as if rejoicing in the true offspring of these doctrines."[2] And yet, there is a great difference between gleaning what is good from Plato's *Republic* and gleaning what is good from *The Wolf of Wall Street*. The removal of all that is false from Plato's *Republic* is a good deal like the metaphor St. Gregory offers, that of circumcision. Removing all that is false from Instagram or *Game of Thrones* requires not a scalpel but a legion of Predator drones.

A "plundering the Egyptians" hermeneutic may be appropriate when dealing with pagan classics, but an honest man will note that for every time God allows His people to plunder their enemies, there are ten times when He does not. Sodom and Go-

morrah are not plundered but immolated. In Acts 19, the Ephesian Christians burn sorcery books valued in the millions. One
may easily imagine that not all the information contained in
these books was wrong, but the slivers of truth were not thought
to be worth the temptation of keeping them around—besides,
were the young Christians to sell their books of sorcery, they
would only have empowered their enemies and made it harder
for them to receive the gospel. The plundering of Egypt takes
place well before the Israelites receive the law that frees them
from spiritual tyranny, after which God is far more restrictive
in what pagan wealth He allows his people to keep. Achan and
all his children are stoned to death as punishment for keeping
a small quantity of gold, silver, and fine clothing from Jericho.
Suffice to say, Scripture by no means teaches that plundering
the wealth of God's enemies is a standard form of cultural engagement.

It must also be noted that Christians who spend a lifetime
plundering hedonistic entertainments for what little good they
contain are much less interested in plundering, say, Virgil's *Ec-
logues*, the *Analects* of Confucius, or any other trying piece of
literature that might actually surrender a good deal of riches.
Plundering the *Analects* is like panning for gold in a California
mountain riverbed. Plundering cable television is like panning
for gold in a Mississippi public pool. Our innate knowledge that
the "plundering" hermeneutic is usually a charade is betrayed every time a dyed-in-the-wool Presbyterian father gets squeamish
about his teenage son reading a contemporary Catholic or Orthodox theology book. All talk of "gleaning" goes by the wayside.
Seduction always begins with agreement.

Seeing

Our confidence in the benefit of asking a few analytical questions at the end of a servile film betrays our genuine ignorance of what eyes are for. The eyes are the seat of judgment. Men are found guilty in "the eyes of the court," not "the nose of the court." The accused is "shown to be guilty" of a crime, he does not "taste guilty" of a crime. Why are the eyes the seat of judgment? Why is sight the king of the senses? Because light is appropriate to the eyes, as sound to the ears and smell to the nose. God does not come to us as "true smell of true smell" or "true taste of true taste," but rather "true light of true light." Because of this, the eyes commune with God in a unique manner beyond the other senses.

And yet, to judge is not the final purpose of the eyes, nor will the eyes be employed in judgment in the life to come. The final gift of God's life to man is the beatific vision, not the beatific taste (though God is bread) or the beatific sound (though God is word). In the beatific vision, the eyes cease to judge and man surrenders to the unmediated experience of God's being. At last, the eyes are opened to receive and commune. In the beatific vision, our eyes surrender, yield, swoon. In this life, the eyes are the seat of judgment; however, on certain occasions, the eschaton spills backward over the dam of time and sloshes into the present, and we are momentarily able to use our eyes to surrender our whole person to someone or something else—or we are able to briefly receive something or someone in return. Often enough, such surrendering happens by sight, by image. It often happens at the movies, though it also happens on headphones, at symphonies, and at museums. We enter a trance of self-for-getfulness, lose track of time, and even lose sense of the fact that the movie, story, or song we are hearing is something other than ourselves.

When Bob Dole was running for president in 1996, he made an offhanded comment about how the film *Trainspotting* "glamorized heroin" use, and all the clever whips cracked the fellow over his remark because scene after scene in the film shows heroin users living in sad and desperate squalor. Dole admitted later that he had not seen the movie, which is unfortunate, because there is a good case to be made for the film glamorizing heroin, even while heroin addiction kills and maims the characters, reduces them to bestial behavior, and so forth. *Trainspotting* is a potent collection of stunning and enigmatic images. The film is so engrossing that it draws the viewer out of his sense of self— momentarily pausing the endlessly looped tape whereby a man's consciousness repeats, "I am a person who is watching a movie called *Trainspotting,*" to his ego—and opens the viewer's eyes to yield and to receive. That the film is sometimes stomach-turning does not undo the fact that it is also bewitching, transfixing, and entrancing, as well. As a young man, I had no interest in trying drugs until I saw it.

When Dante receives the beatific vision in the final canto of the *Paradiso,* he suddenly discovers that he cannot continue writing, and so the Comedy ends. To receive the beatific vision is to present yourself to God and for God to present Himself to you; no words may be used, for words create and imply separation between the speaker and the one spoken to. In a lesser way, something like the beatific vision takes place when the eyes surrender, when judgment ceases, when wonder takes over, when the psychic aspect of a man spontaneously submits to the image before him. Such an image might be righteous, but it is often sublimely vicious. "Did you see how the director was glorifying sensuality in that scene?" The philosophical, ethical speech which follows a stirring scene holds little power over it, for it has entered the soul in a manner which renders it difficult to judge. In truth, the idiot is better suited to forget *The Wolf of Wall Street* than the wise man, for the idiot is not given to surrender. *The Wolf* rolls like water off the idiot's metal heart; however, anyone with a fine education in theology is more likely to wrap the film around the axle of his mind. A world-class athlete preparing for peak performance keeps a limited diet, while moderate athletes can eat and drink what they like. The moderate athlete is accustomed to eating foods which would wreck the performance of a better one. The same is true of intellectual health, as well. Strong minds do not readily let go of potent images. The more righteous the student, the less suited that student is to "handle" wickedness.

Horizontal Comparisons

It is one thing to compare a child to his peers, but it is another thing to compare a child of today with children of twenty years ago. For example, over the past twelve years, I have found art history to be an increasingly tough sell to high school students. When I began my career as a teacher, my students looked forward to days during which we set our books aside and looked at slides of Baroque and Romantic art. Art days were thought a treat. Today, most of my students lose interest in old paintings so quickly that I now dread teaching art history. They have become accustomed to images being funny, sexy, or amusing, needing no more than a single sentence of explanation, and rolling by at a rate of twenty to thirty per minute. Asking them to ruminate on a single image for ten minutes, especially one which is neither funny nor exciting, produces an agitated classroom of students who joke about the paintings to relieve their boredom and anxiety. I should add that I am by no means referring to "bad classes." Even students who earn high grades and write competent essays quickly become bored by old paintings.

What is more, teachers now commonly make remarks to one another such as, "Fifty years ago, if a student failed a test, the student got in trouble. Today, if a student fails a test, the teacher gets in trouble." When garden-variety Republicans hear this saying, they are apt to nod, to shake their heads and bemoan the welfare state, the courts, emotionally fragile millennials, micro-aggressions, safe spaces, trigger warnings, and a world wherein no one is made to take responsibility for their actions. At the same time, I can attest to just how often self-professed conservatives complain that their children's grades are not high enough. The same sorts of parents who complain about the welfare state are also given to complain that their child "has never received a grade this low before." The same parents who mock safe spaces and trigger warnings also write angry emails about how discouraged their child was at "having worked so hard on this project and received so low a grade." The same parents who protest raising the minimum wage nonetheless unsubtly remind teachers their children need good grades to get scholarships. The same Christians who protest the legitimacy of moral subjectivism often complain that a certain grade on an essay "seems very subjective," as though raising the grade would miraculously make it less subjective.

In brief, today's conservative Christian parents often argue that their children deserve higher grades. Within the realm of academia, even Christian academia, just deserts are a thing of the past. Parents who vote Republican nonetheless want the grades their children earn to be adjusted in order to accommodate feelings, disabilities, and disadvantages. A school is not viewed as a place where children go to get educated, but a place where the playing field of society is leveled. Plenty of conservatives are willing to adopt socialist lines of argument if it means their children will materially benefit.

Not Cake, but Poison

A single two-pound brick and four half-pound stones will balance out evenly, but the soul cannot be so balanced. If a man wants to lose weight but also wants to eat cake, he will have to account for those calories by cutting back at meals and exercising more often. However, social media is not like cake or any other fattening food. It is more like methamphetamine or strychnine, and there is no way of balancing out the effects of consuming such things. Poison not only attacks a man's health, it attacks the means by which a man's health is renewed. As opposed to thinking of social media consumption as a heavy rock which must be balanced out by the counterweights of old books, black and white films, Baroque music, and hours spent in a good museum, it is more fitting to think of social media as the heavy rock by which the scales are smashed. The health of the soul is not a recipe that can be doubled or halved. If a man pours bleach into his eyes, he cannot balance the effects of the bleach later by contemplating icons of Christ because he will not be able to see those icons. Likewise, social media is not atoned for in the reading of *Paradise Lost* because social media makes *Paradise Lost* incomprehensible.

Mediocre things corrupt the soul in a way that cannot be fixed through quantity alone. Mediocre things corrupt our desire for good things. The man who accepts mediocrity's offers of pleasure as authentic will simply become more and more frustrated with good things the longer he is subjected to them. A man who willingly blinds himself will not begin to see beautiful paintings simply because he stares at them for long enough. He must be wise enough to not blind himself in the first place.

Endnotes

1. Aristotle, *Rhetoric*, trans. W. Rhys Roberts (New York: Dover Thrift Editions, 2004), 84.

2. St. Gregory of Nyssa, *The Life of Moses*, trans. Abraham J. Malherbe and Everett Ferguson (Mahwah: Paulist Press, 1978), II.40.

11.

Common Things

"The most extraordinary thing in the world is an ordinary man and an ordinary woman and their ordinary children."

—G. K. Chesterton

Between uncommon things and mediocre things, between heaven and hell, between the supernatural and the unnatural, between rewarding challenge and coddling ease, we find common things. The fact that common things are situated between uncommon things above and mediocre things below does not mean that common things are a mixture of both. Rather, uncommon and common have a naturally harmonious and familial relationship, like father and son, while mediocrity is vampiric and attempts to devour both. Common things are minor expressions of the same goodness to which uncommon things bear profound witness. Colloquially speaking, common things are neither holy nor special, but average, typical, usual, predictable, reliable. They are not very good, but good enough.

Nearly every modern industry, business, and human enterprise the world over has an incentive to produce mediocre things; however, the fact that mediocrity may be found anywhere does not mean that most things are mediocre. We are disproportionately aware of uncommon and mediocre things because they stand out from what is common, for common is not simply a qualitative judgment but a quantitative one. Obviously, most things are common. By definition, most things cannot be special.

The fact that most things are common does not necessarily mean that most people like common things, though it certainly behooves a man to have a coherent and livable philosophy of them lest his life be a constant vexation. Were a man to have a few unsavory ideas about the spring equinox or the 1992 Summer Olympics, his life might very occasionally be punctuated with awkward conversations but otherwise roll out evenly. Everyone has a few strange ideas. However, if a man has false, oddball beliefs about common things (like lunch, books, sex, or illness), every day of his life will involve a painful, losing struggle with the cosmos.

Proportions

In the creation week, only one day in seven is holy, which means that most of our lives were meant to be committed to common things. Common things are not a byproduct of the fall, but the good creation of God. The fact that Thursday isn't holy is not a problem, but neither is it a problem that plenty of food, music, and tasks aren't holy. Because holy things pertain to the spirit, they function on a different sort of economy than common things, which are far more concerned with the body. If a man is physically hungry, eating a large dinner will prove more satisfying than eating a small one. However, if a man receives a larger portion of Eucharist from the chalice on a Sunday morning, he is not more holy than the man whose portion was smaller. A couple's marriage will not prove stronger simply because their wedding ceremony went on for three hours. The church has historically prescribed small portions of Scripture to be read every day, perhaps no more than two or three hundred words, but to read a Steinbeck novel at such a pace would be absurd.

Christmas and Common Things

Uncommon things are sufficiently demanding that most people do not have the time or money to make them common. Not only does the separate economy of spiritual things mean that we can make do with far less holy water than drinking water, but the expense of uncommon things prohibits their regular enjoyment. For example, Christmas requires many weeks of preparation and comes with a great cost: purchasing gifts, decorating the house, serving several lavish meals, and so forth. But the fact that Christmas is a burden is by no means a strike against it, for if it were not a burden, the holiday would be easy to neglect and forget. The burdensome nature of holidays means that those who celebrate must begin preparing for them many weeks in advance. Most of the people who complain that the Christmas season is too long are men who have little involvement in the gift-purchasing, wrapping, sending, baking, and so forth. For those involved in such work, the Christmas season is just barely long enough.

Christians have traditionally understood the long period of Christmas prep as common time wherein plain foods are eaten at home and a greater number of church services are held throughout the week which anticipate the Nativity. (At the very least, abstaining from rich foods in the weeks leading up to Christmas is an ancient tradition of the church, though one which has fallen out of fashion in the age of mediocrity.) To some extent, abstinence and renunciation are natural to any sort of preparation, whether one believes there is a spiritual benefit to doing so or not. The tradition of gift-giving requires that we give our evenings and weekends to shopping, wrapping, and taking parcels to the post office, which means we must forgo some of our usual entertainments. The tradition of festal music means that we attend and participate in more performances and services, many of which require extensive rehearsals. All of these labors culminate in December 25th and its twin feasts, one of which is the Eucharist, and the other of which is the enjoyment of festal foods with family and friends.

At least, December 25th *ought* to have twin feasts, but one may intuit that "I Heard the Bells on Christmas Day" is a very old song not only because few American churches still have bells, but because there is no one around on Christmas day to ring them. When I was a child, my family was part of a congregation which acknowledged Christmas and sang Advent hymns before the holiday came, but which did not actually celebrate Christmas in church on the day itself. Thus, on the morning of Christ's birth, there were no holy things to see or hear or taste, just more of the same music and the same food. We opened our gifts and then everyone was supposed to feel happier than they did the day before, although we had no cause to be so happy. It is unreasonable to demand that a person begin acting much happier when you have given him nothing but a little pile of stuff to be happy about.

The first time I became depressed on Christmas, I was twelve years old. This melancholy returned at the end of every December until I was nearly thirty years old, by which time I was married and had a child. It was not until I began treating the weeks which led up to Christmas as common that my melancholy finally went away.

What is true about preparation for Christmas is true of all seasons, though. Gratefully accepting the lesser pleasure offered by common things readies the soul and the body to receive uncommon things, which satisfy a man by uniting his body with his soul. Common things are humble, for they modestly step aside when the time has come for something greater. Common things make no claim to greatness, to profundity, or to transcendence. Inasmuch as common things are deferential, they teach common people to be deferential, as well, and to acknowledge the hierarchies which are natural to mankind. Resistance to such hierarchies leads to hatred of both high and low, great and small. Any society or political movement which despises hierarchies while simultaneously claiming to represent "the people" never secures enough popular support to take power through an election and must resort to violence, terrorism, and intimidation instead, much of which is directed at the people who refuse to support the highly abstract and unproven theories championed by the avant-garde. Progressives have never been able to sort out whether "the people" are ignorant rednecks or enlightened comrades to the cause. In order to love what is common, one must believe in something which surpasses it, for it is that surpassing realm to which love lifts commons things.

Nebraska

Common art is not divine but human, and so it lasts a lifetime.

Like a man, common works of art ultimately pass, but they do not pass quickly. Because we are accustomed to common things, they can seem invisible in a way that keeps us from recognizing their arrival and departure. Common things are worth revisiting multiple times and we can understand them on deeper levels with subsequent revisits, but society does finally get to the bottom of them.

Bruce Springsteen's *Nebraska* is a fine example of common music. One listen is not enough to fully appreciate the beauty of the album, but twenty listens is. Even after twenty listens, *Nebraska* is still enjoyable because the subjects and themes are common, which is to say that the music is concerned with human experience as we encounter it on a day-to-day and week-to-week basis. On an average day, a man has a little time to think about death, desperation, fear, his wife, his children, or his childhood, but he does not have enough time to consider these subjects with great depth. On any given Monday, while driving to the store, a man might consider his whole life, but not with much more contemplation than he would give his wife's proposal that they plant herbs and not flowers in the garden next year. *Nebraska* is appropriate to such days and such depths of consideration. Springsteen's thoughts are not profound, but they do get below the surface, which is often all a man can handle while driving to the store.

Nebraska never inspired a mania, although an interest in the album has been more or less constant over the last several decades. The record is capable of clarifying what it means to be a man born in the twentieth century to blue-collar parents, a common enough kind of person that even those born under different circumstances could benefit from listening to it. But Springsteen's interests on *Nebraska* are pedestrian enough that the record will not likely outlast the listeners for whom the album was intended. Within two generations or so of Springsteen's death, there is a good chance that interest in the record will dry up, as well.

In the age of mediocrity, every adult must come to terms with the fact that the rising generation is largely indifferent to the songs and films that seemed so important just twenty-five years ago. When one considers the most popular albums of the 1970s—Pink Floyd's *The Dark Side of the Moon* or *London Calling* by The Clash—it is difficult to believe such iconic records will ever lose their enduring cool. However, a good deal of popular music from the 1950s now seems quaint, grandmotherly, or obscure. The difference is nothing more than a generation. When cultural artifacts pass the three-generation mark, which is also roughly a single human lifetime, our interest usually begins declining rapidly. Affection for Pink Floyd and The Clash survives because the people who made them household names are still alive, though most of these people will be dead in another twenty-five years. By that point, *The Dark Side of the Moon* will not seem any more cool than the *South Pacific* soundtrack, which was wildly popular in the late 1950s. At three to four generations of removal, the emotional appeal of common things becomes obscure. The Tin Pan Alley pop songs of the early twentieth century make for interesting museum pieces, but they no longer carry much of an emotional pull. They strike modern ears as a little childish, a little cartoonish, even though their intended audience heard them as moving, sincere accounts of the human experience.

All this to say, *Nebraska* will not last forever, but like a good man who honors his mother and father, the record will live long on the earth.

Because it is common, a person may enjoy *Nebraska* without ever feeling the need to read (or write) a book about the album. Many hundreds of commentaries have been written on the works of Dante and Milton, but no one needs a guide through a common book—while commentaries and documentaries about common cultural artifacts can be intriguing, they are not necessary. On the other hand, apart from Dorothy Sayers's canto-by-canto explanation of the *Divine Comedy*, many readers find the poem incomprehensible.

Anyone is free to read the *Comedy* whenever they like. However, were a survey conducted of all the people alive today who have read the *Comedy*, I suspect most of them would report that their first encounter with the poem took place in a classroom, which is another way of saying they were forced to read it. Of those whose first experience with the *Comedy* was not in a classroom, many were likely compelled to read other difficult old books and knew, therefore, that they were capable of both understanding and finishing an uncommon work of literature. The same is true of *Paradise Lost*, the *City of God*, Plato's *Republic*, and a hundred other classic books. It is not impossible for a man who has never been compelled to read old books to suddenly begin doing so, but such instances are unusual. For this reason, if and when American universities finally do away with their classics and humanities departments, reading Homer and Virgil and Milton will still be legal, but almost no one will do it.

The realm of common things, however, is far more subject to the individual's will. When a man moves through the public square, he has little control over what music he hears, what advertisements he sees, the architecture of the buildings through which he passes, or how other people dress. However, when he is at home in the morning or on the commute to and from work, when he has free time in the evening before bed, or when he passes the weekend, then he may fill his time with whatever music, books, films, museums, and churches he pleases. It is here that a man chooses between common and mediocre things.

With a few notable exceptions, mediocre things are not sinful, and so the man choosing between something mediocre and something common is not making a moral decision. Modern Christians are inadequately poised to deal with such decisions, though, because they are obsessed with morality, bored by piety, and always ready to cry "Legalism!" if anyone tells them that they *must* do anything. Against such slow and deficient love, St. Paul tells the Ephesian church they should be very careful how they live and should do everything they can to "redeem the time, because the days are evil" (Eph. 5:16). This exhortation is not given to unbelievers, as though "redeeming the time" might mean "getting saved." Rather, people who have been redeemed by Christ still have a good deal of redeeming to do on their own. Elsewhere in his epistles, St. Paul quotes a libertine slogan popular in the city of Corinth, "All things are lawful," but points out that many things which are allowable are nonetheless worthless. "All things are lawful for me, but I will not be mastered by anything" (1 Cor. 6:12) implies that man may become enslaved to worthless things which are not, in themselves, sinful.

Intellectual Playrooms

Man is free to redeem his time on earth for as much or as little as he likes. It is possible to get quite a lot in return for an hour, and it is possible to get almost nothing for it. We may sell our time cheaply, which is what mediocre things encourage us to do, or we may sell our time at exorbitant rates, which is what things of uncommon beauty demand. To say that mediocre things offer little for our time is to acknowledge that they are useless in the future. And while most mediocre things cost no more than common things, they are expensive in the sense that we tire of them quickly and need a replacement.

At some point or another, everyone has entered a home wherein the children's room is perpetually in a state of disarray due to the fact they have entirely too many toys. But the number of toys has everything to do with their quality. When we imagine children who have too many toys, we intuitively know that they do not have too many blocks but rather too many buzzing, beeping trucks, guns, games, dolls, and action figures, many of which no longer work properly. Though the toys are returned to their bins every few days, they are regularly brought out en masse because the children tire of them so quickly. A child with a hundred flashy toys has no incentive to teach himself to play with one toy for the whole afternoon. Likewise, a man who has slept with a hundred women is always in desperate need of another.

Like wooden blocks, common things offer a fair return on our time. They do not repay outlandishly, but neither are they stingy. The man who cultivates contentment with common things owns less than the man who demands the intense pleasures of mediocrity. A taste for mediocre things ultimately creates a soul which looks like the cluttered playroom of a child with too many toys. The mediocre soul is disorganized and full of broken things which are not worth remembering.

Wanting less has nothing to do with "minimalism," despite cyclical trends which commodify decluttering. Purveyors of modern minimalism do not care whether people tidy their homes and take a few boxes of ugly junk to charity stores, for minimalism is concerned with persuading people to buy new things, particularly expensive, monochromatic things from Sweden which embody the correct aesthetic. Within the minimalist marketing scheme, owning less is always a coy way of justifying one or two more large purchases. If a woman gives ten J.Crew sweaters to Goodwill, she can reward herself with the purchase of a nine-hundred-dollar Jil Sander sweater which "will never go out of style." However, the same people who shell out for items in a fashionable, minimalist aesthetic tire of them soon after the wind changes and the purveyors of cool announce, "Bright colors are back in." Owning less is a fool's errand if it is built on an unsustainable philosophy. There is no shortcut to wanting less—you can't purchase just the right items and then find that you don't want anything more. Wanting less is a virtue which can only be acquired through self-effacing gratitude for the common, modest place in the world wherein fate has decreed that a man should live.

Your Lot In Life

Not all common things are created alike. The fact that two cups of coffee, two dress shirts, or two films are common does not mean they are indistinguishable in terms of quality. In the same way that some holy things are holier than other holy things, some common things are better than others. One may acquire a two-dollar cup of common coffee at a convenience store, a three-dollar cup of common coffee at Starbucks, or a four-dollar cup of common coffee at a privately-owned café. The coffee at the privately-owned café is probably more pleasant to drink than the cheap stuff, but this fact alone proves nothing. Common, uncommon, and mediocre things all offer pleasure, but the pleasure offered by mediocre things is obsequious, sycophantic, flattering, and fawning.

Common, uncommon, and mediocre things may also be found at all income levels. While their many distinctions are not wholly unrelated to money, neither can they be reduced to purely economic concerns. Some mediocre sandwiches cost five dollars, some cost fifty. Some things are expensive but worth it, while other things are cheap but still a bargain. Rich people can afford better common things than poor people, but this does not mean that the rich are necessarily spoiled. Likewise, the rich may long for the mediocre things typical of the poor and the poor may long for the mediocre things typical of the rich. A poor man may be corrupted by the cheap amusements of tawdry YouTube videos, and a rich man may be corrupted by the expensive amusements of weekends in Las Vegas. Suffice to say, mediocrity is not a temptation unique to any income bracket.

Because common things are analogous to nature (and uncommon things are analogous to the supernatural), learning contentment with common things requires that a man accept his "lot in life." However, the idea of a man's "lot in life" is distasteful to most modern secularists, who are constantly trying to eliminate lots, level the playing field of society, and reduce all men to pure will. Any discussion of a "lot in life" also invokes concepts like destiny, fate, and especially luck, none of which sit well with modern Christians, who find the idea of lots superstitious or a challenge to God's sovereignty. And yet, despite our misgivings about whether or not it is just, Scripture teaches us that "God has given riches and wealth to every man, and He has enabled him to enjoy them, to accept his lot, and to rejoice in his labor" (Eccl. 5:19). God has not given the same wealth to every man; however, God has enabled every man to enjoy whatever wealth he has. Of course, while man is enabled to enjoy the wealth he has, he is free to lust after greater wealth, as well. To capitalize on our ability to enjoy whatever wealth God has given us, we must live in such a way that we get a good return on our time and are not mastered by pleasure, be it sinful pleasure or the kind of slippery, shallow pleasure that quickly leads us to neglect our souls.

Society

Regular, intentional, and joyful dependence on common things requires a love of nature—not just the simple pleasures of nature, but the revelations of God's person offered by nature and the beneficial limits it imposes on our wills. The love of nature thus entails gratitude for civilization, which is the ancient and endless project whereby man perpetuates his own existence so that he may continue loving and caring for nature. The continued existence of man depends on both nature and civilization, for without nature man would die and without civilization he would lose his reason for living.

Civilization is not simply the subduing of nature, but the orderly adoration of the God Who reveals Himself in the beauty of nature. Cheese is a way of giving thanks for milk. Wine is a way of giving thanks for grapes. Paper is a way of giving thanks for trees. The cheesemaker says to the cow, "It is good that you exist," and extends the life of the cow's milk. The winemaker says to the grape, "Stay. Make yourself comfortable. Do not leave too soon." As the cheesemaker to the cow or the vintner to the vine, so is the relationship between civilization and nature. A just society—i.e. one which is a local and circumscribable icon of all human civilization—must accordingly balance its own needs with everything that nature can supply, working out an arrangement whereby both parties may carry on indefinitely. This requires a brokering of treaties (so to speak) with the land that the society occupies and with neighboring societies as well.

In the same way that certain cultural artifacts have survived for many hundreds or thousands of years, so, too, many features of society have remained constant over time. Across the centuries, certain lines of work transcend region and religion. A survey of history proves that most functional societies require doctors, farmers, soldiers, lawmakers, kings, judges, butchers, bakers, teachers, executioners, and fifty other professions, but also husbands, wives, sons, and daughters. Each profession, calling, and archetype carves out some small clause in the "primaeval contract of eternal society"[1] (to borrow Edmund Burke's expression) by which every generation negotiates with Mother Nature for the health and happiness of "those who are living . . . and those who are to be born."[2] Each clause constitutes not only some distinct knowledge of Mother Nature, but also a means by which man is suited to interact with the material world. The object of such knowledge is conventionally known as "human nature." To put it simply, every profession produces an insight into human happiness which no other profession can supply. All work is honorable because every conventional human labor reveals God's image in a way which fits necessarily alongside the other revelations. Butchers need bakers, bakers need lawmakers, lawmakers need executioners, executioners need undertakers, and even undertakers need doctors, for unless man lives, he cannot die. Without bakers, the world would be bereft of irreplaceable knowledge.

Given such interdependence, the butcher or baker or painter who doesn't "play by the rules" is robbing society of something important. Frustration with the limits which nature imposes on the will goes hand-in-hand with a distrust of society which is not only witnessed in anti-social behavior like graffiti and rioting, but also in the banal slogans upon which conservatives and liberals alike raise their children. In an Enlightened age, even elementary children are taught to think of "revolution" as the only true path forward, and thus any child who wants to be a good baker must be a revolutionary baker, every good musician must revolutionize the guitar or the drums or the four-minute pop song, every good painter must revolutionize the image, just as every good lawmaker must revolutionize society.

And yet, in a society wherein everyone is trained to be revolutionary, almost no one really *is* a revolutionary. Rather, everyone simply hates the perfectly common thing he becomes.

Endnotes

1. Edmund Burke, *Reflections on the Revolution in France,* Reissue (Oxford: Oxford University Press, 2009), 97.

2. *Ibid.,* 96.

12.

Caveats

I have lectured in defense of tradition for many years, and thus I am familiar with the common objections that old things are racist, sexist, and bigoted. Often enough, the argument against tradition is as simple as this: *Paradise Lost* may be a longstanding human tradition, but so are racism and slavery. Typically, this objection comes from people who have never studied *Paradise Lost*. For the minuscule number of people who have read *Paradise Lost* and still think it racist, a handful of lines from the book might be offered in support of the claim, as well as stray quotes from Milton's other works or his biographies.

No Golden Age

I prefer to answer the idea that "racism is traditional, too," with the quote from Gustav Mahler which opens this chapter. "Tradition is not the worship of ashes" means that tradition is not concerned with resurrecting some long-dead golden age, although confusion on this point is understandable because conservatives speak reverently of "a time when children respected their elders," and "an age when Christianity was honored," and "an era before the feminization of men and the sexualization of children." Progressives are justified to point out that while children called their fathers "sir" back in the 1950s, their fathers were less interested in addressing Black people by respectful names.

"In this world you will have trouble," cautions Christ, which implies that there was no period in the past—no matter how brave the men, how beautiful the art, how prosperous the church—wherein scriptural warnings against the way of the world could be put on hiatus. The book of Ecclesiastes is positively brimming with descriptions of the world as a place where injustice, infidelity, deception, and betrayal are the ever-present backdrop against which all men must work out their salvation. The world was an awful place back in the 1950s, but also during the time of Christ, the apostolic age, and even when funds for the Hagia Sophia were pouring in and the gospel was spreading like wildfire. Violent entertainments were popular in the pagan age, they were popular in the Christian age, they are popular in this confused age, and they will be popular in whatever comes next. "Man is born into trouble," wrote Solomon, anticipating the Carolingian Renaissance just as much as the Third Reich.

When traditionalists look to the past, though, they are not looking at everything that is old. Referring to "a time when children respected their elders" may include the 1950s, but they are not suggesting everything that happened in that time period was good, or that most of it was good, or even that it would be worth it to live with the bad of the 1950s if we got to have the good, as well. Rather, when classicists refer to "the time when children respected their elders," they have less interest in "the time when" and much interest in "children respected their elders." Some children still respect their elders, and the traditionalist is content that such children are both happier and better suited to deal with the world than ill-mannered children.

Though traditionalists often speak appreciatively of "the past," they are not terribly interested in any particular time. In fact, the opposite is true. Traditionalists are interested in that which has transcended time. That a distant golden age is "distant" means it has not lasted, which means it wasn't golden in the first place. Tradition is not "the worship of ashes," and so the traditionalist is content for mankind to collectively decide not to pass certain books, symphonies, plays, and structures on to their children. When bulldozers move in to demolish a football stadium built in the 1980s, no traditionalist heroically stands in the way. Neither do traditionalists oppose buying new socks or replacing chipped plates and saucers. Traditionalists favor what has lasted, not what happens to be around. Traditionalists prize things that last simply because most things don't, and when something does not last, they know that it is usually the thing's fault.

In like manner, slavery is not a human institution that has met widespread, universal acclaim and been handed down from one generation to the next in unbroken succession. Many powerful criticisms of slavery and racism may be found in the writings of the early church fathers, particularly St. Augustine, who drew upon the fact that all mankind was born of a single human body as a sign of the importance God placed on fraternity and unity.[1] In "No Enduring City," David Bentley Hart recounts how the city of Bologna, on August 25, 1256, announced "the abolition

of all bonded servitude within the city's civil and diocesan juris-
dictions," after which the freedom of nearly six thousand serfs
was purchased out of the communal treasury. The city issued
a formal decree entitled *Liber Paradisus* wherein a theological
explanation of the emancipation was offered. Hart translates the
opening of *Liber Paradisus* as follows:

> *In the beginning, the Lord God Almighty planted a paradise*
> *of delight, in which he placed man, whom he had formed, and*
> *whose body he had adorned with the garb of radiance [a shining*
> *raiment], endowing him with perfect and perpetual freedom.*

Summarizing the rest of the decree, Hart writes:

> *It was only by sinning, the argument proceeds, that humanity*
> *bound itself in servitude to corruption; God in his mercy, how-*
> *ever, sent his Son into the world to break the bonds that hold*
> *humanity in thrall, that by Christ's own dignity all of us should*
> *have our natural liberty restored. Thus all persons currently*
> *bound in servitude by human law should have their proper*
> *freedom granted them, for they along with all the rest of us*
> *belong to a single massa libertatis wherein now not so much as*
> *a single modicum fermentum of servitude can be tolerated, lest*
> *it corrupt the whole.*[2]

In the early nineteenth century, William Wilberforce argued
from Christian principles that Great Britain ought to abolish
the slave trade; in the middle of the nineteenth century, Abraham Lincoln relied upon traditional Christian conceptions of
charity and liberality to condemn slavery; and in the twentieth

century, Martin Luther King, Jr. employed Christian theology to attack racism. The idea that every Christian nation defended slavery on traditional grounds until secularists of the 1960s used their newfound confidence in reason to prove the practice was evil for the first time is absurd. Tracing Christian arguments against slavery or racism across the centuries, one quickly discovers that arguments against the practice written in the fifth century and arguments against the practice written in the nineteenth century are easily reconciled. On the other hand, secularists radically redefine racism at very short intervals. The same speech that brings a progressive mob to chant "Blessed is he that comes in the name of the Lord!" one year might easily warrant cries of "Crucify him!" the next.

None of this is meant to suggest that racism is not a problem. But racism is one of many perennial sins which mankind is given to battle over and over again. The fact that racism is an observable phenomenon in nearly any era of human history does not mean it is traditional, for prostitution may also be found anytime, anywhere, and the same is true of drunkenness, murder, rape, and sickness, even though none of these corruptions is ceremonially handed down from one generation to the next. Rather, these sins continually reemerge in society over time. They are sometimes granted legal status (which is yet another perennial sin of mankind) and must be defeated once more, but the way in which prostitution "lasts" from one generation to the next is nothing like the way *Paradise Lost* lasts. Every fall, high school and college classes all around the world will turn again to the music of Bach, the talent of Rembrandt, and the wisdom of Solomon. Their work and thought is perpetually studied, new books and reports on their genius are always being written. Teachers give

their students Bach to play, families travel hundreds of miles to
see the work of Rembrandt, fathers quote the proverbs of Solomon to their children, and this has been the case for hundreds of
years. The means by which prostitution, murder, and racism carry on has nothing to do with the way Bach, Rembrandt, and Solomon carry on. Cancer is not a human tradition, though fighting
cancer is. Slavery is not a tradition, though liberating slaves is.

Idolizing The Past

Defending something so diverse as "tradition" lends itself to contradictions. It is not as though all the old books say all the same
things. Jean-Jacques Rousseau and Edmund Burke both wrote
treatises on politics which have lasted hundreds of years, and
yet the two men vehemently disagree with one another at every
turn. Does the fact that they disagree about so much—and yet
their works have lasted—not prove that something can last and
still be bad?

While transcendence is the most reliable standard by which
to judge the goodness of a cultural artifact, it is by no means
fail-safe. Uncommon things last because they are spiritual, but
demons are spirits, too. So while slavery and prostitution are
not human traditions, *The Communist Manifesto* is, as well as
The Social Contract, for both books have lasted long enough to
enter the canon. We may find less extreme examples of traditional disagreement in the realm of theology, for Protestant and
Catholic theologians of early modernity disagreed strongly and
catalogued their disagreements in books which have lasted long
enough to enter the canon as well.

Having identified disagreements in canonical texts, certain

kinds of scholars are apt to say, "You see, the past is all well and good, but we must be careful not to idolize it." Rather, they suggest, we must carefully and meticulously examine everything from the past, keeping what is good and dismissing what is bad. While this sounds reasonable enough, those who make such claims assume that all men agree on the standards by which the past ought to be evaluated. Even if they did, the standard used to evaluate the past would come from the past, as well. If our standards for evaluating the past do not also come from the past, they must be created ex nihilo every morning. And what standard should we use to evaluate our standards?

Some conservatives claim the Bible is our standard for evaluating the past; however, the Bible is not an abstract set of theories, but a book from which different church traditions are able to derive separate aesthetic, theological, and moral criteria for life and worship. Christ rather plainly tells His followers they should "call no man on earth 'father'" (Matt. 23:9), and yet every sane Christian man refers to the fellow who sired him as "father." By what standard should we judge a man's interpretation of Matthew 23:9, then? A Catholic and a Presbyterian in the midst of a theological argument are forever responding to one another's proof texts with, "I don't think that verse means what it seems to say," because every ecclesial tradition proffers a distinct way of reading the Bible. The New Testament is full of straightforward-sounding claims which are anything but, such as Christ's instructions to pluck out your eye if it causes you to sin, to cut off your hand if it causes you to sin, and to give to him who asks of you and not expect anything in return. All the Christians I have met who blithely claimed they "simply did whatever the Bible commands" had two eyes, two hands, and little understanding of hermeneutics. It is not possible to read the Bible without reading it in a certain way, and our ways of reading Scripture are derived from long-standing traditions. In the same manner, it is not possible to evaluate the past without evaluating it in a very particular light. The idea that everything from the past ought to be judged assumes that our standards spring fully-formed from the mind of Zeus every sunrise. In fact, standards develop no less slowly than the past itself.

In this day and age, the danger of "idolizing the past" is a good bit like the danger of "works righteousness," which is to say that it is not much of a danger at all. Given the profound sloth, laziness, boredom, and ennui of the average American, we are flattering ourselves to pretend that "works righteousness" is a sin to which we are actually tempted. Similarly, the omnipresence of banal, sensual, ephemeral popular culture has placed the possibility of idolizing the past on a very long hiatus. If this nation began making a conscious effort to worship the past, it would take all of us—working around the clock—more than fifty years of robust and tireless idol-making before a single instance of genuinely blasphemous love for the past was possible. Americans loathe the past. Even conservative Christian Americans loathe the past. Anyone who spends an hour reading Burke's *Reflections on the Revolution in France* (1790) will see that fewer than one in a thousand self-professed conservatives alive today have the respect for custom or tradition which served as the ante for conservative political philosophy at the end of the eighteenth century.

Our distaste for the past is well-disguised by claims about the need to scrutinize our history, although it is risible just how little respect must be shown before warnings against idolizing the past are issued. At the slightest hint of nostalgic sentiments, the smallest deference for older manners, the most trivial preference for older films, someone in a crowd will begin reciting a very tired list of our grandparents' sins. Many American Christians think missing church to play soccer is justifiable but would raise a skeptical brow if they heard a fellow believer say, "I oppose cremation because St. Augustine opposed it." If modern Christians were as concerned about not idolizing their fathers as not idolizing their great-grandfathers, a father would not receive so much as a birthday card from his children but rather a slap in the face and a lecture about race and gender. One really must wonder why the author of Hebrews, in the famous eleventh chapter, does not take Noah, Abraham, Moses, Rahab, and David to task for their sins, but simply uses them all as positive examples of faith, worthy of imitation.

As opposed to carefully scrutinizing the past according to an amalgam of standards cobbled together from prejudice, common sense, upbringing, and the passages of Scripture we privately determine to be perspicuous, a man should allow his church to be the standard by which the past is judged. If he does not trust his church enough to judge the past, he should find a church he does trust to do so. If he does not trust any church well enough to judge the past for him, he should simply stop going to church altogether lest some poor Baptist or Lutheran minister be saddled with yet another know-it-all rogue who will split the congregation ten years down the road.

As an Orthodox Christian, the creeds and dogmas I confess have more in common with some denominations and traditions than others. On a good many issues, Orthodoxy has more in common with the Catholic Church than the Presbyterian

Church, and yet, as one who teaches his students to be virtu-
ous through the reading of classic literature, I can do far more
for a strong Presbyterian than a watery Catholic. I would rather have a Presbyterian student who respected his church than
an Orthodox student who did not, and I would prefer that my
young daughters spend time with robust Protestants who believe icons to be damnable idols than with Orthodox children
who believe icons do not really matter. The Christian who is indifferent or embarrassed of the dogmas his denomination teaches will someday be embarrassed of his God. However, obedient
Christians—be they Presbyterian, Lutheran, Catholic, or Baptist—may someday say to the Lord, "I am not worthy to have
you come under my roof, but only say the word, and my servant
will be healed. For I too am a man under authority, with soldiers
under me. And I say to one, 'Go,' and he goes, and to another,
'Come,' and he comes, and to my servant, 'Do this,' and he does
it" (Matt. 8:9). These words were spoken by a Roman centurion,
a servant of Jupiter, and Christ replied that He had "not found
anyone in Israel with such great faith." The Roman centurion
understood the hierarchical order of reality and recognized in
Christ a new sort of authority, one with power over even the
elemental forces of the world. Genuine conversion is predicated
upon just such a recognition.

Every Christian denomination and tradition makes a range of
dogmatic pronouncements on theology and history while also
leaving a good deal to the discretion of its members. In accepting all the dogmas of his church, a man does not forgo the right
to any opinion whatsoever. When a man refuses to accept the
dogmas of his church, however, he makes it clear that any apparent obedience to the clergy is nothing more than an agree-

able coincidence of opinion. For all those matters about which a man's church makes no authoritative claim, he is free to do as he pleases, but he does well to recognize that for an opinion to be valuable, it must be based on something which is not an opinion. A man may base his taste in music, drama, and architecture on the dogmas of his church, or he may base his tastes on lonely, selfish, hermetically sealed-off calculations of what will give him the most bodily pleasure. The Orthodox Church does not force parishioners to choose Mozart over Maroon 5; however, a reasonable Orthodox Christian will consider the music of the Divine Liturgy, which is dogmatically mandated, as well as the iconographic art and architectural design on display in many hundreds of consecrated cathedrals, and understand that while Mozart is not Orthodox per se, his work drafts on an understanding of beauty which is far more harmonious with Orthodox piety than the work of Maroon 5. This is true not only of the Orthodox Church, also but of the Catholic Church, the Anglican Church, and certain denominations within the Protestant mainline. However, it is not true of fashionable, nondenominational churches with nightclub names and rock band worship teams, although such churches often leverage their nontraditional aesthetics as a sign of wisdom and virtue.

Because many Christians believe salvation is an instantaneous, judicial decision made in one's favor, they are loath to see a connection between the way a man feeds his soul on Sunday morning and the way he feeds it the rest of the week. We believe in the separation of church and state, but the modern age has made politics omnipresent, and so the separation of church and state has become the separation of the church from everything else. We no longer believe that the church is a blueprint for reality or even a just society but that secular culture should invent itself, refine itself, critique itself. If we allowed the traditional aesthetics of our churches to inform our tastes, our lives would simply be much less fun, which, for saved people, often arouses suspicions of legalism and works righteousness. There is nothing which evangelicals publicly, corporately petition God for more often than that they would "just have fun this afternoon" or "have a good time tonight." Every barbecue, every sporting event, every party, every game night. Sadistically enough, there are even meetings (wherein no alcohol is served) which open with prayers for "a good time." Saved Americans consistently struggle to conceive of any higher purpose for their gatherings than having fun, which only results in a profound skepticism toward prayer, for everyone knows that God is not necessary in order to have a good time, which means that God has very little to do with music, literature, and so forth.

Origins of Tradition

No small part of the modern Christian's disenchanted view of tradition is born of confusion about where traditions come from. From a rationalist perspective, the material aspects of a tradition are useless after the intellectual origin of that tradition has been forgotten. Tradition is nothing other than a mnemonic device for remembering the past, for what matters most to a rationalist is the mind, and he believes that the way to remember something is to consciously recall it and have nice discussions about the subject. Rationalists tend to have great confidence in conversation—in fact, all the problems of the world could be solved quite quickly and tidily if everyone would just fold their hands and dialog with one another. The problem with liturgy, piety, and tradition is that they distract us from the real solution to the world's problems: polite, reasonable conversation. When traditions lose their reference points, they lose their function as a memory aid and there is nothing to talk about, nothing to preach about, and no way to keep out the inevitable descent into disorganization and violence.

These are certainly odd beliefs for Christians to hold given that, for many churches, the most traditional service of the year is also the most serene. The Lessons and Carols services held on Christmas Eve are reliably more peaceful than annual budget meetings, despite the fact that the latter purports to be nothing more than a reasonable conversation, while the former is an ancient collection of customary songs and texts, none of which is rationally explained before dismissal.

Rationalism, the atheistic cousin of Gnosticism, looks forward to a world of pure mind. If the truth behind the tradition can be remembered without the tradition, we may transcend the tradition. The purpose of everything from Christmas trees to crosses, birthday candles, neckties, handshakes, curtsies, and candy canes is to remind us of some distant truth, but if we can remember that truth without the tree, the cross, or the candles, the symbols are superfluous. When symbols have no inherent value, meaning can be given, stolen, lost, destroyed. All symbols are then ultimately arbitrary, and so we are free to make the Christmas tree a symbol of an anti-Christian holiday if we like, and we are likewise free to declare that—in this house, at least—stepladders hold the same meaning for us that Christmas trees hold for others.

Before going further, though, I should note that rationalism, relativism, and Gnosticism have become far bigger problems for Christians since the World Trade Center attacks than they are for secularists. While secularists presently embrace a nominalist philosophy of gender and hold that a "woman" is whatever I say it is, secularists are presently far more comfortable with the idea of objective truth than they were in the 1980s and 90s. Not too many years ago, secularists were apt to argue that any woman who didn't like abortion shouldn't get one. Today, secularists are comfortable telling those who oppose abortion that they are wrong. Neither do secularists allow that Confederate flags and Confederate statues "mean different things to different people," but rather take a stand that Confederate symbols have inherent, non-negotiable meaning. When I argued about religion with secularists back in college, I was often told, "Don't shove your ideas down my throat." Since then, however, the tables have turned and it is conservative Christians who are now more apt to defend themselves with these words. There was a time when relativistic philosophy stood outside Christian communities and threatened to get in, but Christians have since found themselves the unhappy possessors of relativist philosophies which we struggle to expunge.

If a symbol is merely a set of instructions for how to get to the symbolized thing, ignorance of the language in which the instructions are written creates an unbridgeable distance between the two, and we are thus free to redirect any object to any meaning we like. We could say, "The park is like a church to me, so I go to the park on Sunday morning," or, "Children's bodies have the same sexual value for me that adult bodies have for most other people." The church nave, the body, candles, hymns, architecture, and flowers are all meaningless until we give them meaning, and we are free to change the meaning whenever we like. In this way, there is really no such thing as a male or female body, and neither is there such a thing as a candle or a hymn or a rose. For this reason, it has become de rigueur for avant-garde art to consist of some standard object, like a glass of water, that is entitled "An Oak Tree" and placed on display. It is little surprising that the popularity of nihilistic philosophy followed closely on the heels of rationalism.

Of course, Christians should not let rationalists swindle us with their gruesome, philistine philosophies. In the many centuries before secularism, Christians embraced a radically different, sacramental theology of meaning and symbol. Meaning was neither assigned nor artificial. Rather, meaning was natural, which meant that a thing's nature *was* its meaning, and that meaning could not be lost or gained. It was the work of man to discern the meaning of things. Of course, modern scientists rejected the belief that meaning was inherent and instead channeled all their energies into figuring out how things work.

For medieval Christians, meaning was a cause that brought a thing into being, and so the symbol and the symbolized thing could not be separated. When a man ate a certain food, he ingested the meaning of that food in the same way that he ingested the nutrients of the food. Eating an entire birthday cake will make a man fat whether or not he knows how many calories it contains, and Christians held that meaning was no less objective than caloric content. The ex opere operato view of the Eucharist was not some lonely theological fact. Rather, Christians held an ex opere operato view of the entire cosmos. Every conceivable object was the sacrament of itself.

In *The Meaning of Conservatism*, Roger Scruton argues that

traditions are "a form of social knowledge,"[3] not mnemonic devices which can be disconnected from knowledge. This simply means that Christmas trees, crosses, candles, and so forth are, in themselves, ways of knowing. Scruton writes that "modern liberals tend to scoff at the idea of tradition. All traditions, they tell us, are 'invented,' implying that they can therefore be undone."[4] However, Scruton argues, "A real tradition is not an invention; it is an unintended by-product of invention,"[5] which means that men cannot call traditions into existence. Rather, we merely recognize that traditions have come into being while we were busy doing other things.

The truth of Scruton's claim should be obvious to anyone who has ever tried to invent a tradition from whole cloth. Most traditions are born either of intense suffering or triumph over intense suffering, which is why Christian tradition makes far more of Good Friday and Easter than of, say, Jesus Christ getting left behind in Jerusalem when He was twelve years old. Because so many traditions are rooted in pain, they cannot be created by sheer will (unless a large group of people suddenly decides to seek out great pain just so they can remember it later). But it is not enough to say traditions are "born" of intense suffering, for the purpose of tradition is not to relive suffering, but to redeem suffering and to understand particular instances of physical suffering as touchstones of universal spiritual afflictions. The Christian rite of baptism, for instance, sacramentally enacts the drowning of the Egyptian armies. When the catechumen descends into the waters of baptism, the enslaving power of Satan is drowned out of him, just as the tyrannical Egyptian army was drowned in the Red Sea. When the baptizand comes out of the water, he has become the nation of Israel emerging safely on the other side of the Red Sea. (Footnote: Once again, I am drawing here on the "The Great Rebellion" from David Bentley Hart's Atheist Delusions) A tradition is an event we recall from the past and, upon reflection, believe to be a rare touchstone with the transcendent. Accordingly, we want to relive that event over and over so we may resume communion with the transcendent and steel our souls against eternal death. We cannot force or conjure such communion with the transcendent; however, we may recognize such communion once it has ended.

If there was ever a separation between tradition and meaning (between sign and signified), it was during that dark chasm of history which followed the fall of Adam. However, when the Word was made flesh, an end was made of the merely representative power of words and images and objects. The Incarnation brings together symbol and symbolized, reference and referent, language and object. When the Word was made flesh, the distance between symbol and symbolized vanished. When the Word was made flesh, symbols became doors of entrance into the symbolized. In the Incarnation, the symbol and the symbolized become one another, and so a free movement of being between symbol and symbolized is possible, constant, fluid. The Word made flesh brings together the finite and the infinite, the body of Christ and the Second Person of the Trinity.

For the Christian, nothing can ever lose its meaning. Because meaning is not given, it cannot be lost. Meaning depends neither upon the consent, design, nor memory of man. Meaning depends upon the omnipresence of God and the Incarnation of the Logos, truths which are independent of human desiring. Thus, it does not matter if a man knows where the tradition of the Christmas tree comes from; it is enough that he installs one in his home come December and decorates it. The installation of the tree and the enjoyment of the tree's meaning are synonymous. It does not matter if an infant knows the meaning of food; it is enough that the child eats and does not starve. It does not matter if a man knows why lilies are symbols of purity; it is enough that he brings them to his wife after she gives birth. The man who eats candy canes, decorates a tree, wears red and green, and sings "I Saw Three Ships" enters into Christmas itself. Intellection is not required. The candy cane is no arbitrary symbol of Christmas. The candy cane—like all symbols—is inseparable from its history, usage, creation, telos. The man who eats the candy cane, even if he eats it in ignorance, eats the telos of the candy cane. He gnaws on meaning. He chews history.

Because traditions cannot be suddenly and willfully created, it is more fitting that we view them as natural objects (for which we are merely custodians) than as our possessions to treat however we like. In this way, we might view the *Iliad*, the *Odyssey*, the *Aeneid*, *Paradise Lost*, and Mozart's *Requiem in D Minor* like forests, mountains, rivers, tigers, or any other natural phenomenon. While we have the power to destroy them forever, if we merely take care of them, they will last indefinitely. Forests, mountains, rivers, and tigers possess an inherent power to perpetuate themselves. Likewise, while the perpetuation of the *Iliad* from one generation to the next occurs through effort and sacrifice, our efforts to carry on the tradition of Homer are born of the belief that it should not—and could not—be otherwise. Beauty draws us to itself; thus, we cannot choose what becomes tradition. Rather, we are the amazed observers who find that, year after year and generation after generation, the love of certain things never dies.

At the same time, as our interest in the *Iliad* and the *Odyssey* never dies, we must acknowledge that these books are not merely natural. Rather, they are fitting tributes to the priestly realm, where the immanent is bound to the transcendent, the material to the immaterial.

Endnotes

1. Augustine, *City of God*, trans. Henry Bettenson (London: Penguin Classics, 2003), 502-503.

2. David Bentley Hart, "No Enduring City," *First Things*, August 2013. https://www.firstthings.com/article/2013/08/no-enduring-city.

3. Roger Scruton, *The Meaning of Conservatism* (South Bend: St. Augustine's Press, 2002), 31.

4. *Ibid.*

5. *Ibid.*

13.

How to Choose

"In an age in which the media broadcast countless pieces of foolishness, the educated man is defined not by what he knows, but by what he doesn't know."

— Nicolás Gómez Dávila

Finally, I would like to return to the matter of how we choose what to watch, which is the subject which prompted the authoring of this book. As an art form, film is still so young that speaking of "classic films" is not entirely justified, at least not in the same sense in which we speak of "classic literature" or "classic architecture." It is too early to declare any film "uncommon." Nonetheless, some films are worth watching over and over again, other films are worth several viewings, and many very popular and lucrative films are not worth watching once.

While television and film can be intellectually and spiritually rich, both hold disproportionate sway over our lives. Aside from working and sleeping, modern people spend more time watching television shows and movies than anything else they do; thus, if a man does not employ a coherent philosophy when choosing what he watches, an astounding amount of his life will be wast-

ed. It is the wager of this book that the man who wisely chooses what he watches will invariably watch less, for good things
are both more taxing and more satisfying than mediocre things.
While watching less and watching better will not save a man
from hell, it will enable him to live by standards that transcend
his want of pleasure. Such standards are necessary to the pursuit
of virtue.

Good taste has more to do with what we love than our ability to articulate why we love it. Uncommon art often leaves us
speechless. Epiphanies render mortal men dumb, grasping for
words, or embarrassedly mumbling gibberish. When children
of seven or eight hear a Beethoven symphony for the first time,
they often claim they "like" the music, but when asked why they
like it, they reply, "I don't know." The same is true for many adults
who simply aren't honest enough to say that they don't know
why, so they cobble together reasons based on recollections of
something said by a critic. It is better to adore beautiful things in
uncomfortable silence than to justify ugliness through a series of
dazzling propositions.

The final pages of this book are not concerned with watching
well but with *choosing well what we watch*. I mean for the following
principles to be taken at face value because they can help readers
cultivate better taste in film, but I also mean for these principles to represent the standards by which Christians choose what
books, music, clothes, food, and furniture they buy—even what
churches they attend and what political causes they champion.
In closing this book with a series of exhortations about choosing
what to watch, I do not mean to imply that a man's taste in art
has priority over his beliefs about God. However, if a man's taste
in art is unrelated to his beliefs about God and beauty, he cannot

hope for art to do him any good.

The kinds of things we love often tacitly reveal what we actually believe about God, although we claim otherwise. A man may confess, "The chief end of man is to glorify God and enjoy Him forever," and still live in such a way that an impartial observer would conclude that he believed the chief end of man was to enjoy the world and hope God did not mind. Proverbs such as, "Where your treasure is, there your heart will be also," "The proof of the pudding is in the tasting," and "The Devil is in the details," suggest that the ways we spend our time and money constitute a kind of unspoken creed of their own. I am not asking readers to be skeptical of their church creeds, but I offer the following series of recommendations on choosing films as a way of evaluating all the unspoken creeds by which we live.

Choose in Advance

As opposed to deciding that you want to watch something and then trying to figure out *what* to watch, decide first what you *ought* to watch, then figure out when to watch it. Anyone who believes that he ought to watch something has necessarily accepted the word of another, someone who knows better than he does, for *ought* implies obedience to an authority.

The man who begins scrolling through an endless series of menus trying to figure out *what* he wants to watch is engaged in a pointless mission, for he is simply too embarrassed to admit that his wants are tawdry. If his wants were good, he would not have to spend time trying to figure out what they were. "I don't know what I want to watch" allows a man to pretend that he would watch something good if only a sufficiently excellent

option would present itself, though all he really wants is something sensational. The desire for good things is not something
we suddenly find within ourselves, as though virtue and good
taste emerge apart from our knowledge and then lie dormant in
our souls until the possibility of watching Krzysztof Kieślows-
ki's *Dekalog* awakens them. Rather, we must tremble and struggle to want good things.

The man who wants to watch "something" scrolls past one
good option after another but justifies his lack of interest by
claiming that he is not in the mood for those films; in truth,
he is bored and does not care to find a sustainable, intellectually healthy way out of his boredom. The man who hears that
Tokyo Story is good and makes plans to see it does not want to
escape boredom, but ugliness. The man who goes off in search
of "something" to watch is under the mistaken belief that his
wants will reveal themselves when he finds a movie which looks
good and can easily relieve his boredom—but because no such
movie exists, the search continues until he is willing to let one of
his two criteria go. Of course, the criterion he usually abandons
first is that of goodness, after which he is likely to resort to the
most immediate and destructive relief for boredom there is: pornography.

It is possible for a man to plan to see a film simply because
he has heard it is very grotesque, very violent, or that an actress
he fancies removes her blouse during a certain scene; however,
if these are his only reasons for planning to see the movie, he
will be just as happy with a different film that features the same
lurid content. On the other hand, if a man plans to watch *Tokyo
Story* because he has heard it is good, he will not be content to
watch a different good movie because goodness is personal to

the things which possess it. Goodness cannot be added to or subtracted from a thing in the way that violent spectacles and nude bodies can. In like manner, the man who intends to marry a certain good woman is not content to exchange her for another simply because they are both good. Goodness is so personal, in fact, that the man who falls in love with a certain righteous woman may readily pass up the chance to pursue an even more righteous one. Because the pleasures offered by evil are physical in nature, they can be easily substituted, replaced, or faked. But good things do not contain goodness in the same manner that a cup contains water. Goodness is the manifestation of a thing's nature, and doing away with a thing's goodness means doing away with the thing itself. Wickedness is a corruption, though, which means we may easily imagine a thing with or without it.

To put it simply, wickedness is just not that important.

Choose Films You'll Watch More than Once

Making the most of your time in the manner that St. Paul teaches means abstaining from one-night-stand relationships with films. Before deciding on a certain film, a man should ask himself how many times he is likely to watch it. If he is only likely to watch it once, he is also likely to forget about it quickly. If he knows he will only watch it once, he has already admitted to himself that the film will not be very good.

Before a man of twenty-six decides to watch a certain film, he should ask himself whether he wants to watch the same sort of films when he is thirty-six, forty-six, or fifty-six. If not, there is no reason to watch it now. If a man knows he would be embarrassed to watch something ten years down the line, his present interest is not spiritual, but carnal. If he does not believe a film will do him good ten years down the line, there is little chance it will do him good now. Goodness does not change so quickly.

Watch Films You Can Trust

Many Christian writers who discourse on cultural engagement exhort readers to sharpen their analytical faculties while watching movies. Because Hollywood is corrupt and most films are moral minefields, the Christian viewer must enter a movie theater with a heightened sensitivity to the subtle lies of his spiritual enemies, learning not to fall prey to seduction, deception, and the overthrow of his own heart. While a good deal of this is true, I suppose, it is only applicable for Christians who have no sound criteria for choosing what they watch and instead see whatever is new and popular because it is new and popular. Anyone who pays to see a film he believes to be a moral minefield is a poor steward of his time. Why watch such a film when good films are readily available?

If Christians content themselves with films which are widely praised for their beauty, films which are recommended by friends and trusted critics, there is no need for viewers to suspiciously analyze everything they see and hear. Neither is there a need for heightened sensitivity to the potential for lies, deception, seduction, and invitations to unbelief or apostasy. When a film has been vetted for decades and approved by people we trust, we can turn off the analytical faculties of our brains and surrender so that the film can shape and mold our hearts. Good art requires a passive audience, an audience willing to quit talking, to quit thinking about what it wants, to quit trying to impress other members of the audience, and who simply receives the work with simplicity of heart.

Very few films deserve such an audience. Most films deserve suspicion, but then most films are not worth watching.

Watch in Silence

Nothing is likely to disturb Christians who think cultural engagement is important quite like being told to turn off their brains, be quiet, and surrender to something, no matter what it is, for many of the same Christians who believe moviegoers need to carefully pick apart movies also believe congregations should double-check their Bibles every Sunday to make sure that what the pastor preaches is true. No one is trustworthy.

However, receiving good art with humility means admitting that the artist is more interesting, more wise, and more creative than one's own self. Worldview analysts are generally unwilling to admit this for any film, while sympathists admit it too easily. The idea that most films, especially most new ones, are not worth watching is offensive to worldview analysts because it means that some films *are* worth watching and that such films require a passive audience. The idea that most new films are not worth watching is offensive to the sympathist because he believes that the adoration of popular culture is the surest bridge by which he can reach the lost.

By contrast, the humble audience member does not regard himself as an important part of the equation, as though his opinions were equally valuable to the art he receives. Great art is chiefly concerned with heavenly communion, not strengthening earthly community, and thus good art requires long, quiet contemplation. This is disheartening to modern Christians, who want to voice their opinions about every little thing, for this is what the secularists they admire spend all their time doing.

Great art usually requires a good deal of time to truly understand and appreciate it, which is why it is unwelcome in societies with high cultural metabolisms.

Be Willing to Be Called a Snob

The reason Christians subject themselves to "moral minefields" is either because they believe saved people ought to have as good a time as possible while waiting to die, or because moviegoing allows them to keep a finger on the cultural pulse, which better enables them to present the gospel in a savvy way to unbelievers. Cultural engagement presumes a voracious appetite for news and entertainment, which invariably grants priority to fashionable things. If Christians want to have better taste, it will mean falling behind the times. It will mean having nothing to say about the most important books, films, and music of the moment.

If Christians are willing to struggle in order to love things that last, cultural engagement will not necessarily go away. Rather, better taste reimagines cultural engagement as something other than think pieces on gospel hunger in rap records or worship services which are TED talks crossed with all-ages emo concerts. Any Christian who wants to love things that last, any Christian who wants to join "the democracy of the dead" and escape "the arrogant oligarchy of those who merely happen to be walking about," as Chesterton once put it[1] should be prepared to be called a bigot by secularists and a pretentious snob by many of his brothers and sisters in Christ.

Better taste supposes that unbelievers might rather find Christianity a refuge from mediocrity than a mirror image of the garish slums and carnivals they need to escape.

Consider the Calendar

While Americans tend to choose what they watch in an entirely arbitrary manner, consider what it would mean if the opposite were true. Suppose that movies (and the time to watch them) were in short supply and that in the coming year, you could only watch twelve. Let us also suppose that before the coming year begins, you must—like a farmer considering his fields—decide what you will plant, although you are not sowing seeds in the soil but sowing stories in your soul. You are free to plant what you like, but you must decide well in advance what that will be, purchase your seed, and then commit yourself to the project.

Within this hypothetical scenario, then, let us suppose that before the year begins, you must decide how many of the twelve films will be ones you have already seen and how many will be new to you. For instance, you may choose to watch ten movies you have already seen and two you have not. Or eight you have seen and four you have not. Or, you might choose to watch twelve movies you have already seen, or twelve you have not.

Once committed to a certain number of films you have seen before, suppose you also had to choose the titles and the day of the year on which you will watch each. If you choose to watch *Die Hard* again next year, you must decide the month and day on which you will watch it. The same is true of *It's a Wonderful Life*, *Some Like It Hot*, and every other movie you have already seen and choose to watch again. Let us also suppose that for

every new film you allot yourself in the coming year, you are free
to choose the title later, but you must choose the day in advance.
Thus, before the coming year begins, you already know that on
July 12th or August 6th you will see a movie that is new to you,
but you may decide which one when the day arrives.

While this hypothetical scenario might seem strange, it merely involves making a plan to do something which is very important to modern people but which never receives a second thought.
While television and film shape our beliefs and desires, most of
us have no idea how much we watch and put little thought into
what we choose. Making such a plan seems odd at first, but upon
a little reflection, we realize that the idea is not so much odd as it
is daunting, given the embarrassing quantity of shows and films
we thoughtlessly sit through.

Anyone who chooses specific dates on which to watch his
twelve films during the coming year would not choose randomly,
as though any numbered square on the calendar were as good as
the next. Instead, he would choose significant days, maybe even
holidays, days on which he knew he would be free. Having cho-
sen significant days, though, he would also be likely to choose
films which coincided with that day's significance.

Knowing in advance what he will watch (and when) also allows anticipation to play a role in how he conceives of his leisure
time. Anticipation is a memory of the future, the intellectual
shaping and reshaping of an event which also synergistically re-
shapes the heart. The man who anticipates a thing experiences it
a thousand times before experiencing it once. In those thousand
experiences, he lives inside the event, discovers the corners, is
given room to speculate, perhaps even goes through shades of
disappointment and prepares himself to forgive the thing for its

inadequacies. The eagerly-anticipated event is usually so ideal-ized that it is easier to enjoy once it is over; the event itself passes as a dream, a vision, and becomes an even more profound source of enjoyment and mystery in retrospect.

What emerges from an arrangement wherein movies are cho-sen a good deal in advance is not simply a plan, but a way of living which drafts on the greatest revelation of time's redemp-tion—the church calendar.

Coda

While I believe Christians with good taste make for better evan-gelists than Christians who believe that becoming "all things to all men" entails submission to the latest fashions, loving what lasts is not ultimately a strategy for spreading the gospel. It is a strategy for believing the gospel.

When St. Paul teaches the Colossians to "set your minds on things that are above, not on things that are on earth," he is not implying that heavenly things and earthly things are naturally at odds with one another. Rather, as Christ teaches, only God is good—and yet God reveals His goodness in creation, which is His generous gift to mankind. Creation naturally directs us toward the Creator, though man may abuse God's gift and bend creation away from God and back toward itself, which is what mediocre things do.

Uncommon art clarifies and magnifies creation's natural incli-nation toward the Creator, which is makes great art something of a gauntlet, albeit one worth running. Uncommon art binds heaven and earth while mediocre art confuses the two. C. S. Lewis once said, "The joys of Heaven are, for most of us in our present condition, 'an acquired taste'—and certain ways of life may render the taste impossible of acquisition."[2] Common art prepares us for uncommon art, and uncommon art prepares us for the halcyon joys of Glory. God has gifted a few great artists with the power to acclimatize us to heaven. We must use their help to begin acquiring the taste for Glory now.